THE RELEASE

THE RELEASE

More Tales of
Families, Fishing, and Faith

William J. Vande Kopple

William B. Eerdmans Publishing Company
Grand Rapids, Michigan / Cambridge, U.K.

Published 2009 by

Wm. B. Eerdmans Publishing Co.

2140 Oak Industrial Drive N.E., Grand Rapids, Michigan 49505 /

P.O. Box 163, Cambridge CB3 9PU U.K.

Printed in the United States of America

14 13 12 11 10 09   7 6 5 4 3 2 1

Vande Kopple, William J.
    The release: more tales of families, fishing, and faith /
William J. Vande Kopple.
        p.   cm.
    ISBN 978-0-8028-6467-3 (pbk.: alk. paper)
    1. Michigan — Fiction.   2. Fathers and sons — Fiction.
    3. Fishing stories, American.   4. Christian fiction, American.
    I. Title.

    PS3622.A586R46   2009
    813'.6 — dc22

                                    2009030389

www.eerdmans.com

Contents

Acknowledgments

Some of the pieces included in this collection originally appeared in other publications. And some appeared in a form slightly different from the form in which they appear here. It is a pleasure to express my gratitude to the following editors for help with these pieces:

- Thanks to the editors of *Perspectives* for help with a part of "Hope for a Full Recovery."
- And thanks to the editors and publishers of *Summer: A Spiritual Biography of the Season*, by Gary Schmidt and Susan M. Felch (Woodstock, VT: Skylight Paths Publishing, 2005), for help with "Bright Hope."

Preface

Perhaps the most important question for me to answer about this book has to do with how the world of the stories collected here relates to the world in which I, even as I write this sentence, am charging boat batteries in anticipation of opening day in Michigan for walleyes, pike, and muskies. So let me be as clear as I can be: The fishing lures mentioned here are real. The fishing techniques I detail here are real. The people involved in the actions here are real (although I have altered the names of some friends and acquaintances). And the places I describe here are real.

In fact, I truly hope that you will be able to visit and fish many of the spots that I write about. If you have never explored the seemingly endless rapids of the St. Mary's River near the Canadian Soo, I hope that at some point you will have the chance to do so. Ditto for the channels and bays in the Les Cheneaux area, near Hessel and Cedarville in Michigan's Upper Peninsula. Ditto for the boulder-studded stretch of water called Musky Pasture on Little Vermillion Lake south of Sioux Lookout, Ontario. And ditto for the Backchannel of Eagle Lake, far to the west in Ontario. I'm tempted to invite you to try to find the deserted logging camp that is the setting for the decisive actions of

"Trying to Make Up," but I'm not sure I could find the camp myself anymore — at least without my brothers' help — and I would not want to play a role in your getting lost in that wild territory in the U that the Tahquamenon River forms.

But is my memory perfect for everything my relatives and I said and did twenty or ten or even five years ago? No. Are any of the activities in these stories represented from the slant of anyone but myself? No. And do I sometimes embellish aspects of stories? All of my relatives would say that I most assuredly do.

Still, the arcs of connected actions in these stories are true to the nature of individual members of my family, to the ways we generally relate to friends and one another, to the way we interact with the natural world, and to the memories we have carried away from outdoor experiences.

I am thankful to Wanda, Jon, Joel, and Jason, as well as to my extended family. As I worked to put together this sequel collection of fishing tales, "the core of my emotional support came from my immediate and extended family," as I noted in the preface to my earlier collection of stories, *The Catch*. "From them came most of the questions or little rubs from which stories grew. From them came reminders about and refinements of memories. And from them came much of my knowledge of and appreciation for stories." In both my nuclear family and extended family, we tell one another some really good stories.

Further, I am grateful for the supportive environment for student and faculty writers created by my colleagues in the English department at Calvin College. When I started teaching at

Calvin, it seemed to me that we in the English department focused mainly on helping our students critique aspects of human culture. But in the last several years, I believe we have also emphasized contributing written works to human culture, and that emphasis has been deeply sustaining for me.

Further still, I am grateful for supportive comments from the larger Calvin community and from church communities that I know. Again and again, all these folks have reminded me about how important it is for a writer to have readers — supportive, interested, inquisitive readers.

My editor for this book, Reinder Van Til, made very important contributions to its final shape. It is unfortunate that only a few people will likely ever know the details of these contributions. For he came up with ideas for revisions of particular stories and for the overall organizational scheme of the book, ideas that made me think, *Yes. Exactly. Why didn't I think of that?*

Finally, I wish to thank Bill Eerdmans, Mike Van Denend, and Gaylen Byker for their encouragement and support throughout this project.

PART ONE

Fathers and Sons

Trying to Make Up

My memories of that Saturday morning back in the fall of my tenth year are vivid but probably all out of order by now: the dew-slickened grasses in that field up near Hoxeyville soaked our jeans to the knees and above as we worked our way through them, pausing now and then to scan the edge of a distant cluster of pines for a hiding place, a natural blind. That thunderclap of a bird — we were sure only that it wasn't a pheasant — had to have erupted not from the ground but out of it. Otherwise, we told each other, we would have stepped on it. We were surprised that our dad, once we had tucked ourselves in among the pines, could relax enough for a little snooze, dozing off with his head on a small mound of pine needles he had scooped together while we kept watch on the field spread out before us, one of us responsible to look left, one straight ahead, and one right. The sounds coming from behind the distant ridge were louder than any I imagined as possible from an animal native to Michigan, and it was not until a buck — at least six points — appeared on the crest of the ridge, staying just out of range of a shot, that I knew what had been snorting. And on the tailgate of our pickup I had my first cup of coffee, which I could never have finished had Dad not slipped me three extra packets of sugar.

My dad had taken me and my brothers, Bob and Bruce, along with him and some of his friends on a bow-hunt for deer. Dad carried his bow and his quiver with about a dozen arrows; in sections of a small rucksack he had a thermos, some dark bread and cheddar cheese, a compass, and a portion of a map. Every twenty minutes or so he would stop and check his bearings. We boys carried our Swiss Army knives, Calvinist Cadet canteens, and some hastily mixed gorp. Once during our hike, after we had left the sopping field, my dad asked us if we could find our way back to the truck on our own, and the three of us considered the question for a few seconds, and said we thought we could. Then we pointed in three different directions.

Very soon after that day, financial stresses, many of them associated with Christian-school tuition for the three of us boys and for Barb, the youngest, became so severe that they moved from the margins of concern to the center of discussion within our family. Every other Friday night after supper, Dad would line up on the kitchen table all the bills that had accumulated, and he'd fret about whom he absolutely had to pay in full and who might accept a partial payment — maybe even a very small one. Mom would pace from the kitchen into our seldom-used living room and then back, toweling the same dish over and over, worrying aloud that sooner or later the financial pressure was bound to strike him as similar pressures had struck several of his friends — with a heart attack.

"Can you believe that — heart attacks at forty-five or forty-six? Whoever heard of fatal heart attacks in men so young? And some of those guys were health nuts. They were always taking fish-oil pills and chewing sunflower seeds. But ach! — all those widows in our church, widows with a bunch of young mouths to feed." The four of us kids would feel more than ordinarily guilty if we had outgrown our church clothes or if a trip to the dentist had shown that we needed a filling.

The practical upshot of all the financial stress was that my dad started accepting any possible overtime at Clare Tool and Die: fifty hours a week, fifty-five, maybe even more. Beyond those hours, he started his own business in our basement: he set up shop with workbenches, lathes, and drill presses so that, in whatever time he was able to squeeze out of the week, he could build surgical arm boards for a local medical arts supply firm. For several years after that Saturday hunting expedition when I was ten, Dad had no spare time to take my brothers and me on deer-hunting trips or anything like them. (Barb had been too young to go with us that day, and as she grew older, she made it clear that going into the woods to kill innocent animals was not something she would enjoy, though she made that judgment without having had any actual experience.) In fact, it was not uncommon during those years for us kids to see Dad for only a few minutes each day, usually in passing, often just before we went to bed.

Years later, when the financial pressures had lessened somewhat, after he actually *had* suffered the heart attack my mother had always fretted about — it was a matter of festering family debate how much it had been caused by all the earlier stress and extra work — he never felt comfortable heading out to remote places like that field up near Hoxeyville. He wanted to have quick access to proper medical care should he start to show signs of heart problems; he didn't trust traveling too far from a major hospital and its cardiac-care unit.

I have some memories from before that Saturday of being in the outdoors with my dad, such as the time when I went out fishing with him on Hess Lake and he hooked and then hauled out of the weeds and muck a pike barely twenty inches long, a fish I'd now shake off my line or let thrash near the side of the boat in hopes of attracting a muskie, but that then seemed like the clearest example of a miracle I had ever witnessed. I also have memories from before that Saturday of being outdoors with my dad and Bob, memories of times he would take the two of us along to the outdoor archery range, where we would stand silently behind him as he drew, aimed, and shot, and where we were then expected to help him claw through bushes for any of his arrows that had somehow managed to miss the target. And I have several memories from after that Saturday of being outdoors with Bob and Bruce: before the three of us got married, we spent several summer weeks backpacking and bushwhacking, from rockslides on Mount Katahdin to dry streambeds in the northern Cascades. But the memories I have of that Saturday deer hunt are the only memories I have of being together in the outdoors with all four of us — my dad and my two brothers.

To be honest, I don't really remember resenting my dad's busyness and absence back when he had to work all the time. And I don't believe that the memories of our day in the field festered in my mind in any way, at least on levels I was conscious of. In fact, with all I had to adjust to in junior high and then high school and then college, I don't think I spent too much time thinking about that Saturday up north.

But after the three of us boys had moved out of the house (Barb was going to college in Grand Rapids and still living at home), I took a week near the middle of August following my first year of teaching to visit Bob in the Upper Peninsula, where he had a short-term contract with the U.S. Forest Service to do some botanical surveying in the Hiawatha National Forest. The first night, as we sat around at his campsite feeding pinecones to the increasingly hungry fire, he surprised me.

"What's your best memory of Dad from when we were little?"

"Why do you ask? What brings this up?"

"Oh, nothing special, really," he said. "It's just that on this job I'm by myself in the woods and fields most of the day, and my mind wanders sometimes."

"I can see that," I said. "I don't know how you stand it, tramping around out here every day. I think I would worry about getting lost. And I'm not sure I'd be comfortable being alone that much."

"I think about lots of stuff from when we were younger."

"Best memory of Dad, let's see. . . . It could be that time I had to tell him I drove his station wagon right into that chain across a rear driveway at West Catholic High School, and he didn't throw a fit, not even a little one. He was mainly concerned about whether I was okay or not. Or maybe when he decided to dye his hair and the process got messed up, and he walked around with orangish hair for a week or so. Or maybe that time we went body-surfing with him and Uncle Bill in those monster waves up at Luding —"

"You know what mine is?" Bob said. "Mine's the time you and Bruce and I tagged along with him that morning he and his buddies went bow-hunting up around Hoxeyville. I'm guessing he would have been shocked if he had gotten a deer, and the three of us probably weren't anywhere near old enough to handle seeing a deer hung up in the field and gutted. But that whole day tramping around and waiting to see deer! Do you remember that bird we scared up? And some of the ferns along the road near where we parked were amazing, like they were out of some Tarzan movie. But the best part for me was hiding in those pine trees waiting for deer to show up in that field — all that whispering, all our jumpiness about every little sound, while Dad just took a short nap, that buck snorting up on the ridge and acting as if it knew exactly where we were. And somehow at the end of the day Dad led us right back to our truck. It was magic. It was all magic. That's got to be one of the best memories of my life."

"I haven't thought about that day in years," I said. "But you're right — that was great. That was more than great. My heart about popped some ribs when that bird took off like it was between my feet. And then Dad turns to me and whispers something about whether or not I needed to change my underwear. I thought, *My underwear? Why's he talking about my underwear, anyway?* Mom was always so afraid we'd get in an accident somewhere and have dirty underwear on that she made us put on clean underwear every morning."

"We absolutely have to do something like that again," Bob said.

"Go hunting together? I think you know that's crazy. Bruce is the only one of us who ever goes on hunting trips anymore, and there's no way you could call what he does hunting. I'm almost positive he couldn't shoot a deer if his life depended on it. He's even told me that more than once he's had a good shot, but then passed it up. His friends have talked about how hard it is to stare down into those huge brown eyes and then finish the thing off. Bruce isn't really into hunting. He just has relatives on the other side who are, and he likes being with them at deer camp — the hikes out to blinds, the big meals, the stories, the jokes, the card games, you know."

"That's probably true, but I'm not saying we have to hunt. I'd just like to get the three of us together with Dad and do something cool outdoors."

"You can't believe how good that sounds," I said. "But how are we ever going to find the time? You know how busy we all are."

"We don't need to plan anything really long — maybe just driving somewhere Friday night, have all day Saturday out together someplace, and then home again on Sunday."

"Well, when are you thinking about — sometime next summer?"

"No way. Think how long it's been since that day we went hunting. What is that, about thirteen or fourteen years? I don't want to let much more time go by. We might not have all that much time left. Let's figure something out for now — this fall."

"Funny, but as school was winding down this past spring, my colleague Dave kept telling me I should use his family's cottage sometime. They have a place on Lake Superior's Whitefish Bay — specifically Pendills Bay — close to a place called Dollar Settlement. Nothing fancy but comfortable, he says, framed by birches on a bluff above the bay. His family goes there every summer for the month of July, but before and after that it's usually open, and he said I'd love it there."

"Sounds perfect. Why don't you ask him if we can have it for a weekend this fall, say the end of September or early October? As soon as you find out, let the rest of us know. Dad can't decline because there's not a good hospital around, since we'd only be twenty minutes from the Soo. And Cheboygan and Petoskey aren't all that much farther away, and they have good hospitals, too. I have a gut feeling that this is going to work out."

"Okay, I'm sure Dave'll say yes, but what are we going to do once we're all up there?"

"Why not have a little contest?"

"All grown up and we still have to compete? Did you ever think that maybe I've never recovered from all those arm-wrestling contests you used to challenge me to?"

"If we don't compete, how do we know who wins?"

"Yeah, yeah, I'm sure it makes sense to you. So what kind of contest do you have in mind?"

"Well, I was thinking that each of us could come up with some ideas for stuff to do in that part of the U.P., and when we all get up to the cottage, we can discuss all of our ideas and then take a vote. All of us should have a bunch of great possibilities to bring up. Don't forget that Dad spent a ton of time in the U.P. when he was younger — and he probably remembers all of it. Mom says that his memory of what he does on vacation is so good that, even after fifteen years or so, he can tell you to the tenth of the mile how far it was that he followed some two-track before pulling off, parking the truck, and then walking to some remote agate beach. So he definitely should have some ideas. Plus, Bruce spent a couple of summers working for the Forest Service throughout the U.P. Even if all he did was work, as he claims, he would have heard about some stuff from his co-workers and from the managers of hotels where they stayed. For me on this job, once I'm out of the field and in a forest service office or having a meal at Toivolu's, I'm constantly meeting people who know about all kinds of good places to visit and things to do in the U.P. And if your colleague is up here for a month every year, he should have plenty of ideas for you. This should be great: we come prepared for all sorts of stuff and then choose one thing when we're at the cottage. Maybe we could even choose a couple. It'll be the Vande Kopple version of living in the moment."

"Okay," I said, "I'll talk to Dave about the cottage. And I'll let you guys know about dates. But I'm not sure I'll be able to come up with any ideas for things to do."

I said it, but it was really one of those little lies that we all hope to be able to get away with. It was easy for me to think of possibilities for outdoor recreation in the eastern Upper Peninsula, and all of them revolved around what I had come to see through my teenage years as the greatest pleasure in the outdoors — fishing. No, I wouldn't have a problem coming up with stuff to do. My problem would be that my dad and my brothers would probably need some unusually strong forms of persuasion to choose fishing, especially over other good possibilities.

My dad included himself among those people — the vast majority, he always claimed — who believed that no one who fished ever actually caught anything. Sure, he'd tell me, I could make a decent case for getting away and having some time for meditation while on the water. I might justifiably be fascinated by the multitude of life forms I could see in various lakes (he had himself spent parts of whole days drifting in a canoe through the shallow coves of Lost Lake in Ludington State Park). With his background building molds and dies, he could understand that I might be intrigued by poured plastic lures and their performance. And he admitted that he understood how I could get a kick out of seeing cottages from the lake side, their good side. But, Dad would unwaveringly insist, so-called anglers never caught any fish. Ever.

Fishing had been ruined for him by my grandpa, who everyone always said had built up within himself about as much stubbornness as a human being could. According to my dad's accounts, my grandpa would take him out to Cranberry Lake, rent a boat, row to the edge of some lily pads, bait his and my dad's line with chunks of crawler, add bobbers, toss out the lines, and then wait. If over time the fish didn't break down and take one of their offerings, my grandpa's response was simple: wait some more. He was certain the fish that could outlast him had never been spawned. This was long before the time of handheld electronic games and iPods, so there was little for my dad to do but stare into the distance and pray that the whole experience would end before he began to suspect he was a victim of child abuse. As my dad grew older and got his driver's license and his own car, he took up golf.

I also knew that a fishing proposal would be a tough sell to my youngest brother. For one thing, Bruce, a gentle spirit from his youth, hated the idea of inflicting pain on any creature. I'm sure that's why he passed up all shots, no matter how easy they were, when he went to deer camp. And that's why he would disagree with me when I would say that catch-and-release fishing causes no real harm. "Sure," I'd admit, "sometimes the fish gets a little tear in its lip, but what's the big deal? I've heard they have hardly any nerve endings around their mouths. And I'm sure those tears heal up."

"Hardly any?" Bruce would scoff. " 'Hardly any' means there are some, and some means there is pain. What do you do when you unhook a fish, tell your conscience to take a nap?"

Bruce's trouble, in my view, stemmed from the afternoon I took him out on a little bayou at Ludington State Park. I had rigged him up with a small hook, half a worm, and a bobber. After I had tossed his bobber and bait out, I started getting my own rig ready, but in the process I took my eye off Bruce's bobber for too long. He had seen his bobber disappear under the water, but didn't know exactly what he was supposed to do, and thus he gave the hungry bass so much time that it ended up gut-hooked. I knew that if I yanked that hook out, I would take a good chunk of its gullet with it. So I cut the line as close as I could to where it disappeared down the fish's throat and then, holding it upright in the water next to the boat and hoping it would be able to rely on its own power, I released it. The bass struggled mightily to swim away from us but eventually rolled over on its side. Again and again we rowed over to that fish and tried to revive it. After its most energetic attempt to swim away on its own, an attempt that took it nine or ten feet from our boat, a gull swooped down from behind us, grabbed the fish, flew away another twenty-five or thirty feet, dropped the fish back into the water, and began pecking at it. While we were trying to drive the bird off by throwing sinkers at it, it pecked out one of the fish's eyes. That ended our day on the water, and if Bruce ever fished again after that day, he never told me about it.

All those in my extended family who have ever fished have been primarily catch-and-release anglers, especially with the real trophies, particularly the muskies. Primarily catch and release, but not absolutely. We will occasionally keep a few walleyes or northern pike for the table, provided no one objects. But since that day at Ludington, we knew that Bruce would object, so we never killed fish when he was around.

My chances of selling Bob on a fishing excursion were probably better, if only a little. He knew that people actually caught fish. And he knew a lot about bodies of water; at one point during his teen years he had even built his own small speedboat. The trouble was that he never kept his or any other boat in one spot long enough to toss out a lure and catch a fish. There was always something farther, something off in the distance, something else beckoning him. He was driven to seek and explore.

If you don't believe me, just hop in whatever kind of watercraft is available to you and Bob sometime, take some fishing gear along, check out the water you're on, propose that you stop long enough to make some casts, and see how he responds. Carry a canoe with him above the dam on that little creek in the interior of Drummond Island so that you have access to the Potagannassing Flooding. Paddle off to the east for a hundred yards or so, and you'll see some of the best-looking pike water you've ever been near.

"Bob," you'll hiss, trying to keep your enthusiasm from making you sound irrational, "let's stop here and run some spinnerbaits through this stuff. Cabbage like this has gotta be full of pike."

"Maybe so," he'll respond, "but right now we're in what's called First Lake. There are three more lakes connected to this one — Second Lake, Third Lake, and Fourth Lake — and if we want to see them all, we've got to keep moving. You don't want to miss any of them, do you?"

Or launch a canoe or a two-seater kayak some spring a couple miles upstream from the mouth of Ontario's Agawa River and start paddling with the current. Soon you'll notice stretches of gravel, and on or near beds finned out of the gravel, you'll see steelhead, perhaps three or four males lined up behind a female.

"Bob," you'll say, pointing downward, "you see those fish? Backpaddle a minute while I rig up and drift a yarn ball past them. If the female doesn't take, I'm sure one of those males will."

"Don't you know where we are?" he'll ask. "If we keep moving along downstream and then paddle north along the coast of the bay, we'll be able to see some of the best pictographs in all of Ontario. Backpaddle? You've got to be kidding me. Compared to those pictographs, what's a steelhead?"

I really wasn't naïve: I knew I would have a hard time persuading my dad and brothers to choose fishing as the activity on our upcoming outing. But I also knew that one or more of them might get so busy that they wouldn't have time to come up with any ideas. A little less competition wouldn't hurt my cause. And one who believes in anything as deeply as I believe in fishing never really gives up hope of making converts, even within his own family.

It turned out that my friend Dave was happy to let us use his family's cottage for the last weekend in September, and Bob, Bruce, and I were able to get away for those few days. After we sent Dad some information about the hospital in the Soo, he agreed to give our plan a try. Dad, Bruce, and I arranged to meet and then travel together from the south, and Bob would make the shorter trip east from his research camp in the central Upper Peninsula.

Once we had all arrived that Friday night, had thrown our gear into bedrooms, and had explored the beach a few hundred yards in both directions from the cottage, we gathered around the kitchen table to enjoy some cheese and crackers and decide what we would do the next day.

"So," said Bob, trying to sound like a game-show announcer, "you all heard how we set this up, right? We were supposed to come prepared with some ideas for stuff to do tomorrow, and now it's time to get those ideas out and vote on which one is best."

"I thought," my dad replied, chuckling, "that with all this assembled brainpower we'd have enough to think about even if I didn't come with any suggestions. You guys have a bunch of ideas, right?"

Bruce shrugged. "I've been so busy lately that most of the time I haven't even been sure what day it is. So I didn't make a list, but I probably could think of a thing or two now if I had to. Do I have to? What about it — did you guys come up with anything?"

"What a bunch of slackers!" I said. "Do Bob and I have to do all the homework? Well, as it turns out, I did come up with some stuff. In fact, I have three different ideas, and they're all pretty good, if I say so myself, and since you're not saying anything, I will say so myself: They're all pretty good."

"We'll be the judges of that," Bob said, pulling a folded paper out of his shirt pocket. "Let's hear what you've got."

"Okay, when was the last time you felt awe, not the cheap modern-day variety, but true awe? Be prepared. Here's idea number one. Just down the road to the west, several streams flow into Pendill's Bay. One or two of them are partially diverted into the trout hatchery, but the rest flow free and wild, and all of them, so Dave tells me, have stretches of good trout water. We don't have to worry about fly rods and special flies. I've brought a bunch of spinning gear, and if we work little spinners along the logs and below the riffles, we're bound to get into some rainbows. If we stay till around dusk, we should find some browns."

"Have they had good rains this summer and early fall?" Dad wondered.

"Rains?"

"Yeah, have they had consistent rainfall the past few months?"

"Not sure — I haven't paid any attention to that. How about over where you've been working, Bob, to the west?"

"Pretty dry, mainly," Bob said, "but I haven't heard much about what's been happening over here. It could have been different."

"Well, anyway, here's idea number two. Just a few miles down the road toward the Soo, there are several resorts on Waiska Bay. The locals call it 'Whiskey Bay.' Dave said almost all of those resorts have boats available, and we could drive over there, rent a couple of boats, and head out into the bay for pike, which I've brought some heavier lures and equipment for. This is the option that would probably put the least strain on Dad. Dave's heard of twenty-pound pike coming out of that bay, especially down in the reeds toward Brimley State Park."

"How long ago was that?" Bob asked, tapping the folded sheet of paper in front of him with his index finger.

"Don't think he ever said anything about dates. But everyone knows that just about every bay of the Great Lakes holds some big pike. And this is Superior, right? The bigger the lake, the bigger the —"

"Okay," Bob said, cutting me off. "That's two ideas. You said you had three, right? What's the third?"

"Well, the third one is really a two-in-one. If we wanted to drive east a little farther than Waiska Bay, we could head to that little park south of the power plant in the Soo and cast into the St. Mary's for pinks and kings. They should be close to the peak of their run. I'd be surprised if not much is happening on the Michigan side of the river, but if not, we could cross over to the Canadian side and fish parts of the rapids. Some stretches there are accessible, even if you don't have waders — we'd be standing on boulders along the river's edge. A lot of the spoons that we would throw for pike, especially the pink and green ones, would work for salmon, too, so we should be all set."

"That park just below the power plant?" Bruce asked. "Isn't that where they had a problem with fish kills? Fish being swept into the turbines? Or am I thinking of the pumped storage plant north of Pentwater?"

"They might have had a problem here," I said, "but I think

they've taken care of it. Grates or screens — stuff like that. So we won't have to worry about snagging any shredded fish. Well, what do you think? Three pretty good ideas, huh?"

"You did your homework, that's for sure," Dad said. "But it looks like Bob has something to offer, too. We can't decide until we hear all the options, right?"

"Absolutely," I said. "All right, Bob, bring it on. You wanted a competition, you've got a competition. What's on your piece of paper?"

Bob unfolded his sheet of paper very methodically, smoothed out the wrinkles in it, and pushed it toward the center of the table. It was part of a topographical map.

"I heard about this from a guy I've gotten to know a little. Sometimes I eat supper with him at Toivolu's. Everybody calls him the 'crazy Finn' — not exactly sure why. Anyway, for years his family has owned a hunting cabin on the land inside the big U that the Tahquamenon River makes. See? Right here. From his hunting cabin, he says, a footpath leads roughly two hundred yards to a small pond. And if you start at the extreme northern edge of that pond and travel exactly seven degrees west of north for a mile and a half, you'll come out of the woods and find the site of a logging camp that's been abandoned for more than a century. The camp is entirely on his land. And he says that the camp has never been touched, so anyone who knows what he's doing should be able to find bottles and axeheads and winches and what's left of saws and stuff like that. Anything we find, he says, we're welcome to keep.

"The thing is, he says that the country we'd have to hike through is confusing — turn any which way and it all looks the same. Of all the people he's told about the camp and given the green light to go look for it — I guess there've been six or seven parties — no one has ever managed to find it. And one group got themselves seriously lost. I was thinking we could drive to his hunting cabin, be the first ones outside his family to actually find the camp, and then do a little archaeology. It should take most of the day. So what do you think?"

As Bob looked up, he was almost exhaling eagerness. I knew that this was the kind of quest he got up in the morning for.

I could tell that Bruce was eager as well: he had pushed his seat forward and was studying the map intently. He had a college degree in forestry, but when he and Judy got married, they had decided to live in Grand Rapids, where forestry was not really a viable employment option. So whenever he could get out in the woods, he once told me, it felt as though he could fill his lungs again.

"In the past I've found more out-of-the-way stuff than this camp," he said now, apparently trying not to stir up any discord. "What do the rest of you think?"

"How far from here would we have to drive before we started the hike?" Dad said, gesturing toward the map.

"It's not that far," Bob replied, realizing what was on Dad's mind. "The crazy Finn's hunting cabin is only another twenty minutes or so to the west. And all on pretty good roads. We'd still be really close to the Soo."

"And how big of a hike did you say it was?"

"Only about a mile and half. I don't think it's going to put a big strain on anybody. The reason people haven't found the camp in the past is not that it's so far from the hunting cabin, but because they didn't have good compass discipline. Bruce and I can handle that, right, Bruce? And in the past few years you've said more than once that you're in the best shape of your life — all the walking, the adjustments to your diet, the Lipitor. And don't you usually carry nitro pills with you, just in case?"

"Yeah, I always carry some with me — in case of chest pain. But you're right, I haven't had any trouble in quite a while."

I could tell that Dad was starting to approach Bob's and Bruce's resonance to the challenge. I could have gone back to my descriptions of the fishing options and added more detail or repeated parts of them with more enthusiasm, but I sensed that nothing was going to make much difference. And although I didn't say anything about it, the challenge of finding that camp was something I resonated to as well. So when Dad turned and gave me the look he had when he desperately didn't want to hurt any one of his children, I thought it would be best for me to be gracious. So I jumped in before he had a chance to get any words out.

"Well, you all know I love to fish. And up here we're near some of the best water anywhere. We're near water that authors people read in school have written about. But I have to admit that it would be cool to be the first ones outside of the Finn's family to find what's left of that camp. I'm fine with trying that tomorrow — if you really want to."

"I think we've pretty much voted," Bob answered. "Let's make sure we get an early start."

My favorite walks in the woods have always been those when I don't have to worry about catching a toe and tripping, rolling an ankle, or getting my pants or parka snagged. I want to walk and look up, studying the subtle beat the trees' crowns are swaying to, trying to understand bits of the hushed messages they are passing down the line.

But after we left the north shore of the Finn's small pond the next day, with Bob and Bruce sharing the lead, followed by me and then Dad, I realized that this was going to be a hike where I wouldn't dare lift my eyes above the level of my shoulders. It turned out to be an hour and a half of sweeping live branches out of the way and trying to pass them on to the next person in line without an accidental release and a lash to the chest or face; of breaking off dead lower limbs, always trying to leave just a stub but sometimes producing a cluster of dagger-like splinters; of straddling one or more blow-downs while stretching out gingerly with the lead foot to make sure our bootplants were not on exposed roots or logs that were slick with moss, or that would shift and roll under even light pressure; of stopping every thirty or forty yards so that Bob could chop a blaze, the whole set of which we would follow on our way back, so that we wouldn't have to keep constant watch on the compass; and, unexpectedly worst of all, of swiping at filaments — could they all have been thrown out by spiders? — that hung invisibly between branches and that we caught on our foreheads, across our noses, and even, when taking heavy breaths, in our mouths.

As much as I could, I tried to keep an eye on how Dad was doing, checking to see how often he stopped and rested hands on knees, how frequently he had to use the back of his sleeve to wipe his forehead, how many times he slipped one hand to the other wrist to get a quick reading of his pulse. I don't think anyone blamed Bob for false advertising: he would have had to presume too much in responding to the crazy Finn's invitation or would have had to take the practically impossible step of making an exploratory visit on his own to know that the mile and a half that we were trying to cover was more like a hacking struggle through a special-forces obstacle course than a renewing stroll in the woods. And as far as I could tell, Dad was doing as well as any of us. Anyway, I knew better than to suggest that any of us turn around, because one of Dad's top-three sayings to us when we were kids was, "If you're a Vande Kopple, you finish what you start."

And then, suddenly, we broke through into the light, into lush green, onto the edge of a large meadow with the heavy atmosphere of long-abandoned dreams and desires.

"No bushes or saplings," I said. "There's nothing other than grass growing in the whole place. You would think that by now the woods would have started reclaiming its own."

"Soil compaction," Bob responded as if he had seen many clearings like this before. "Have enough people tramp over a piece of ground long enough, and you won't be able to get a bush or tree to grow for a long, long time — longer than this place has been hiding here. And this place has been here a long time."

"So where do we start?" Bruce said, placing his compass back into its cloth case.

"Let's walk down the middle and see whether we can tell how many buildings were on this site," Bob said. "I've been in a few camps like this farther to the west, and usually you can see where the wooden foundations were — they'll be mound-like, low, and a couple of feet wide."

As we moved into the center of the camp, it was surprisingly easy to see how the camp had been laid out.

"If you want," Bob said, "we could each take a different foundation and probe along it with a knife to see if we find anything interesting. Take this structure as a starter. This looks like it was the biggest building, probably the main bunkhouse." He knelt near the foundation, stabbed the earth just outside it with his army-surplus knife, cut a line through the sod toward us, removed the knife, and stabbed again, deeper this time, and that's when we heard him hit and break some buried glass object.

"Shoot," he said, looking up quickly, "the Finn said we could dig the place up as much as we wanted, but this doesn't feel right. It seems like this camp hasn't been disturbed since the lumber crew harvested the last trees and moved on. This whole clearing is an unspoiled time capsule. Somebody's gonna want to study this camp sometime. Probably some historians from Lake Superior State College or Northern Michigan University. And they'll come in with the right tools and do the job the way it's supposed to be done, not muck things up the way I just did. I think we should try not to disturb anything."

I agreed with Bob about leaving things be, but I still felt a jab of irritation. "So then what? Are we just supposed to turn around and hit the endurance course all over again? I'm not sure I'm ready for that."

"Naw," said Bob, "we've got some time to play with here. I think we can find stuff to check out right around the camp."

Bruce agreed: "I'd like to take a closer look at those stumps we saw on the way in, back a ways. Didn't have much time on the hike. Can you imagine what those white pines must have been like? Or better yet, can you imagine what this whole area must have looked like with trees like that towering everywhere? I haven't seen stumps like that anywhere else except around Grayling."

"I'd come along," Bob said, "but I want to search the perimeter of this camp for the dump. All camps like this had a dump, and I won't do any real damage to the historical record if I rummage through the garbage a little. Anybody want to come along? Dad, you feel like helping me find the dump?"

"Nope. I think I'll stay right here and rest up a little. I'm starting to feel a little twitchy in my leg muscles — a bit crampy. That hike in took more out of me than I thought."

Bob turned toward me: "How about it? There's probably gonna be some cool stuff in the dump."

"That wouldn't be too bad. But show me the map a second. Is there any water around here? I wouldn't mind checking out some water."

"There's a thin line of blue not too far to the east. It starts a little south of where we are and runs north toward the Tahquamenon River."

"How far off, would you guess?"

"Quarter mile tops."

"That's it then. I'm out to find that stream and see whether it has anything swimming in it."

"Okay, take my map and compass. I'm not going to get far enough away from this clearing to need them. See you in a while — say an hour or so. Try not to get lost."

When I broke back into the clearing after my short excursion, Bob and Bruce were sitting close to the center of the camp, both gesturing energetically. Dad was lying on the ground about fifteen yards behind them, the back of his head resting on one of the foundations, his hat covering his face, his hands folded over his stomach.

"So?" I asked Bob and Bruce as I came up to them.

"Pretty cool," Bob said with a little whistle. "Pretty stinking cool."

"Really? How so?"

"Well, Bruce made some rough measurements of stumps and did some ring-counting, and he thinks that the pines that were cut around here had to be about as big as any cut in Michigan during the logging boom."

"The trees here must have been just unbelievable," Bruce said. "I'm gonna have to do some checking to see how they might have compared to those harvested in the northern Lower Peninsula. And I'd like to come back here someday to take accurate measurements. But I was glad, for the time being, to take a better look at those stumps."

"And I did find the dump — it's out in that direction," Bob said, pointing northwest. "Only about twenty yards past the edge of the clearing. And as far as I can tell, nobody's been in there messing with it. Dozens and dozens of bottles — little green bottles, little blue bottles, little clear bottles — and almost all intact, with their names molded into the glass. You would think hunters would have found the place and blasted everything to shreds — or sherds. Sorry, couldn't resist. The most common ones were labeled Hinkley's Bone Liniment. And my favorite was a pain expeller that was supposed to be good for rheumatism, gout, neuralgia, and colds. I was tempted to take one or two home with me, but then I decided I really should leave things more or less the way I found them. Better for the historians, I figured. But someday I'd like to spend more time just poking through the stuff that's there. Anyway, Bill, I see you didn't get lost — at least not for long. Did you find some water?"

"Some very cool water," I said. "Not long after I started east, I broke out of the kind of stuff we struggled through this morning and found some relatively open ground — a pioneer bush here and there and in the distance a wave of alders. I knew they had to mark water, and they did. It's a little stream only three or four feet wide. Perfectly clear — you could drop a dime in it and read the date. And cold. I splashed some on the back of my head, and my neck muscles tightened right up. After a bit, I noticed the gurgly rhythm of a riffle near me. As I came up to it, I thought I had floaters in my eyes, but then realized I was seeing sudden swift shadows in the water. Brook trout shadows — six of them, eight of them, maybe nine. I followed them upstream as fast as I could, they darting from one overhanging clump of grass to the next, me clawing and clumping my way through alder branches. And they led me right to a kidney-shaped pool with a spring bubbling in its center. But do you think that once I was there I could find those brookies anywhere? They had guided me along and then disappeared. We've got to come back here sometime so I can figure out how to sneak up on some of those brookie ghosts and catch them."

Bob took the map back from me. "Maybe you found the source of that stream. The map just shows a thin blue line starting out in the middle of nowhere. I'd like to head east right now and check out that spring for myself, but we're gonna have to start back to the hunting cabin. We better wake Dad."

"I'll get him," Bruce offered, scrambling to his feet and starting over toward Dad. I was going back over some details about the pool and spring with Bob when we heard Bruce rasping toward us: "Guys!"

"What?" Bob and I responded at almost the same time.

"Get over here. Get over here right now! Something's wrong here. I called him as I walked over, and when I got here I shook him by the ankle — first gently but then a little harder. But he hasn't said a thing. And he hasn't moved. This is bad. Dad!"

Bob and I came up next to Bruce and started our own chorus, both of us on the edge of panic:

"Dad, Dad, come on now. We know you can hear us. Come on."

"Time to head back to the cabin, Dad," Bob said. "We've got to get back. Come on! If this is supposed to be a joke, it's not that funny. Not funny anymore, Dad. Wake up now. It's time to get moving. Dad! Please, Dad, please!"

And just as I took his cap from his face and was starting to lean over to listen for his breathing, his right hand twitched, his eyes came open, and he pulled on my shoulder as he sat up.

"What's all this? Talk about a racket! Thought you guys were all off looking for stuff."

"You had us worried, Dad, really worried," I said, handing him his cap.

"I was gone. I was in another zone. I laid down here, found some moss on one of these foundations and put my head up, covered my eyes, and haven't felt so relaxed in years. Wish I could fall asleep like that at night. But what time is it getting to be?"

Bob glanced at his watch: "Almost six."

"Whoa! A little late, and this time of year the days are getting mighty short. We'd better get moving. We've got some serious ground to cover before dark, don't we?" ✆

Bright Hope

When my dad mentioned at breakfast on the next-to-last day of our family vacation that he was going to drive down to Grand Rapids to bring Grandpa Abe up for a half day of fishing, my little brothers and my sister didn't even seem to hear him. As they raced through their cereal, leaving small puddles of milk on the table with a Fruit Loop or two floating in them, all they talked about between their annoying crunches was getting out on the dock. There they would do what they had done for hours every day of the week so far: lie as quietly as possible on their stomachs and peer over the edge waiting for minnows and small sunfish that they tried to catch by violently and swiftly swooping down on them with partially torn butterfly nets.

But Dad got me wondering. Why would he drive from our rented cottage on Hess Lake to the city and back, later having to repeat the whole process — making it four thirty-five minute drives in one day. Couldn't Grandpa do what he had always done before? He'd always driven his tank-like Deuce-and-a-Quarter — along with Grandma Reka when she was alive, and by himself after she died — to spend part of a day with us while we were on vacation. I sensed, though, that I had better keep my questions to myself. Dad seemed fidgety, scraping at his lower lip first with one eyetooth, then the other, and I knew if I asked any question at all, he might respond with what I hated to hear: "Thirteen years old and already a worrywart! When are you going to quit picking at things?"

When they got back to Hess Lake from Grand Rapids, I was in the boat making sure everything was set. I had three life jackets stowed in a little compartment in the bow. I had a cushion laid out on each seat. I had Dad's metal tackle/toolbox under the middle seat and my plastic tackle box under the rear. I had a Johnson's silver minnow snapped on my rod, and I had checked my drag.

But Grandpa didn't carry his rods and tackle box directly out onto the dock and claim his favorite spot in the bow of the boat, as he always had in the past. Instead, he brought his gear to the edge of our beach, gave a plastic pail a nudge with his foot, and then turned to look for a lawn chair on the grass. Once in a chair, he seemed to be scanning the opposite shoreline, but I noticed that after a few minutes his head slumped forward as he fell into a snooze.

After I had double-checked that everything was ready in the boat, I called to Dad and Grandpa.

"Hey! Are we going to get out there or what? I've been waiting all morning. Not too many water skiers right now. And the big bass are going to be insulted if we don't pay more attention to them than this!"

So Dad walked over and nudged Grandpa, whose head jerked up, and they gathered his gear and came out to the boat. I was surprised to see that Grandpa accepted some help from my dad in stepping down into the boat.

"My hip is pretty much a dud," he said, wincing. "Before I get too old, I guess I'll have to see about getting it replaced."

Once we were all settled in the boat and Dad had rowed us out of the shallows, Grandpa's unusual behavior continued. In the past he had always wanted to take full charge during fishing excursions, telling us that he knew precisely where all the fish were and what they would bite on, directing my dad to position the boat according to his very specific directions, insisting that he get the first crack at casting to spots that he claimed held fish.

But this time, when my dad asked him where he wanted to try first, all he said was, "Oh, anywhere out here past the weeds. It's all about the same." So we drifted along the outside edge of the coontail, and I got busy casting to little pockets in the weeds. Dad made casts, too, but very casually, as if he would be surprised to catch anything. But all Grandpa did was snap on a three-hook plastic night crawler and then lob it out behind the boat. More than once we told him that he needed to add some weight to his line and clean off his lure. We could see the crawler dragging about six inches below the surface only ten feet back of the boat, a couple of brownish weeds snagged on the rear hook. But he left the fouled crawler where it was, resting one spotted hand on the gunnel and staring down at the tiny whirlpools our keel stirred up as the wind pushed us along.

I fought and lost two nice bass in the first twenty minutes or so — it was the most action with big fish that I had had the whole week up to that point — and then Dad asked Grandpa if he wanted to keep drifting.

"You don't have to stay out here for my sake," Grandpa said. "Bill got into some fish. And you said you might have had a hit or two. It doesn't seem to be my day. We might as well call it quits."

So we reeled up and headed in.

When we were tied up back at the dock, Dad gave Grandpa a hand getting out of the boat and then turned to grab equipment from me. As he did, he saw that I had noticed how wet Grandpa's seat cushion was. Some of the liquid had run off the cushion onto the seat itself.

"I'll get a rag and wipe it all up," I said. "No one has to know anything."

"Good. Thanks. He's not been doing too good the last month or so. And you can't believe how embarrassed this makes him. He refuses to talk about it — even to me when it's just the two of us."

"But he'll get better before too long, won't he?"

"This is tough business, Bill. We've been to more than one doctor. And the last one says he's pretty much run out of treatment options."

"But summer's just started, and Grandpa and I usually fish together a lot in the summer. Don't tell me I won't be able to get out on the water with him before school starts up again."

"You know what we say in this family about hope."

"Hope? You mean that line you say and sometimes even sing to yourself?"

"Yeah. Do you understand it?"

"Some of it, I guess."

About thirty years later, long after I had graduated from rented rowboats to my own fishing boat, I occasionally found myself sharing it with one or more relatives — usually adolescent male relatives. At the end of one August, our extended family spent a long weekend camping at Mullet Lake, and during lunch of the first day, my three sons — Jon, Joel, and Jason — and their two cousins — Tim and Matt — started some intense conniving to get me to take all five of them out to try for pike on the flats of the Indian River, which they had heard noticeably successful fisherman talking about at the fish-cleaning house.

My sons knew that I was nervous about having five young boys fishing together with me in the boat. So for the first couple of days I don't think they were too surprised when I put them off and pretended to have no interest in fishing a big new lake. I left the boat on its trailer the first day, then took all the women out for a ride checking out cottages the next. But those boys had worn me down more than once in the past, and they knew they could probably wear me down again.

"What's the point of having a boat called a 'fishing machine' if you don't even use it to fish?" Joel called from the edge of our campsite, where the five of them were taking turns juggling a soccer ball the afternoon of our last full day.

"Yeah," Jason added, "earlier this summer you told us this lake had pike and muskies down by the Indian River, and why would you say that and then not take us out to try for them? Doesn't the Bible have verses about parents not frustrating their kids?"

"I'm just afraid," I said, "that having all five of you together in one boat is trouble, and that starts with a T and rhymes with P," I countered.

"Real funny!" Joel said. "What's *The Music Man* got to do with taking us out in the boat? You think you can trick us by just sitting there quoting lines from songs, but you're wrong."

"I'm wrong?"

"Just think about it a little, Dad," Jon said. "We talked to Tim and Matt about this trip already this spring, and they were so sure they would be able to try for pike that both of them went out and bought some new lures. Would it really be fair to lead them to spend money for tackle they weren't going to be able to use?"

"Oh, I don't know. Is that true, Matt? Did you spend some of your own money on new lures?"

"I bought a couple. I've never caught a pike in my life. Not even sure I've seen one, except in pictures. And Jon, Joel, and Jason got me going with all their stories about your last trip to Les Cheneaux. So I took some of my lawn money and bought a big Rapala — and a red-and-white spoon. The package says it's guaranteed to catch fish."

"How about you, Tim?" I asked.

"I bought a couple of new spinnerbaits, but if you really don't want all of us in the boat with you, I'll try to find some other time to use them. I think my uncle on my mom's side has a canoe." He ended with a little shrug of resignation.

It was the shrug that did it. I could handle their sass and sarcasm; I could handle their arguments, in which they said the same thing over and over, increasing the volume with each repetition; I could even handle most of their whining. But I couldn't handle somber resignation. So I decided to take the chance and say yes to all six hundred fifty or so pounds of them, probably over the limit of my boat's carrying capacity.

And, in truth, they were close to angelic as we headed away from the campground launch site south to the flats, the bow of the boat burrowing into the backside of one swell after the next.

But once we got there and started rigging up to fish, they began to show clear signs that when the five of them were together, tomfoolery or danger or both were never far off.

Joel and Jason liked to take big shiner minnows, position a jackknife on their spine behind their gills, slice their heads off at an angle, hook the decapitated bodies on jigs, and then cast and retrieve the jigs. This, we all knew, was a very effective technique. The slanted cut on the shiner bodies would make them wobble enticingly in the water when retrieved slowly, and if there were any pike around, they usually could not resist such offerings.

The trouble started when Joel and Jason began to argue about who had made the most effective cut. As the argument developed, they started tossing bloody shiner bodies from one end of the boat to the other for inspection. While this was going on, the muscles in my neck and shoulders started to tighten up, because every few seconds I had to look around and do some quick dodging to avoid being hit by the bloody body of a shiner. Alert as I was, I still ended up with a stain on the shoulder of my T-shirt.

When those two saw that the others had finished snapping on crank baits and were ready to fish, they finally decided to drop their squabble and get their baits in the water. But then my neck and shoulders tensed up even more. None of these kids was very big. Jason and Matt, the youngest, were only around five feet tall. But both of them were using rods six feet long or longer, and in order for them to get their baits a ways out from the boat, they would swing the rod behind them to eight or nine o'clock and then whip it forward and release the line.

If they had had a wiffle ball attached to the end of their line,

I probably would have worried only a little about getting bopped in the back of the head. But since they all were whipping out over the water either a large jig hook or a lure with a pair of treble hooks, I feared having one or more hooks rip into my neck or the back of one of my ears. Probably, I thought, the older boys could take one of my ears right off.

"You've got to watch each and every back cast," I warned. "No exceptions! Else somebody will need to have hooks cut out of the back of his head — and you sure don't want that someone to be me." To their credit, they worked hard to cooperate. I could see them glancing over their shoulders to make sure they had a clear lane for their back casts.

Until one of them thought he had a strike. Then they all went into a casting frenzy — *whup, whup, whup, whup, whup* — their rods slicing the air as they raced to land a lure on the spot where they thought the fish had been. No attention to their back casts. No worry when a lure brushed through somebody's hair. Nothing but annoyance about wasted time when one of their lures hooked my baseball cap and took it sailing out over the water.

Sometimes — usually just after one of these casting frenzies had flamed itself out — one of the boys, now feeling the effects of having drunk thirty or forty ounces of Mountain Dew in the last hour, would balance himself up on the gunnel and noisily hit a spot in the water seven or eight feet away. Once one started, another usually followed, setting up a contest about who could hit the water farthest from the boat. The others would estimate distances and declare a winner, who would then sing out in a husky falsetto, carrying across the water, "Pop, pop, whiz, whiz. Oh, what a relief it is!"

After the song, they usually moved into a bragging and joking contest. A few of their jokes were clever; a few, I thought, were just plain stupid. Several approached the ribald, with allusions to parts of the human body that the youngest boys, feeling somewhat awkward between childhood and early adolescence, clearly had not settled on names for.

I should have stopped them, I know, but they were almost manic in their attempts to one-up each other. Plus, I was pretty sure that no one in any other boat or on the shore could hear everything they said. And some late-developing part of my character, I have to admit, actually enjoyed some of their jokes. In fact, I often had to turn away and fake some coughing to cover my laughter.

As anglers say, we really got into some northern pike that night: everybody fought and landed at least a couple. I had several razor-thin slits on my fingers from handling so many pike and getting too close to their teeth. Jon caught his biggest fish of the summer, a thirty-seven-inch northern with such broad shoulders that he and Joel together had trouble holding it still while I took my pliers and got the hooks out.

As we plowed our way back to the launch site, I reminded the boys that since we had to pack up in the morning, I was going to trailer the boat that night and pull it to our campsite. Later, when I had finished backing the boat up next to our tent, I jumped out and told them: "I've got to hit the bathroom before I do anything else. You guys make sure you've got all your equipment out of the boat and do what you can to clean things up. Pick up all the bits of loose line. Don't leave any empty pop cans in compartments. And make double sure there are no hooks lying around!"

As I came back from the bathroom, Jason finished cramming a life jacket into one of the boat's side compartments, whispered something to his brothers and cousins, and walked up to me.

"We were wondering. We know it's the end of summer and you'll probably leave the boat in the garage as you start fishing the rivers for salmon whenever you have time on the weekends, but —"

"But what?"

"Well, we all had such a blast out there tonight — do you think you'd be willing to take the five of us out on the water again when it warms up next spring? It would stink if this was a one and only."

"You know what we say in this family about hope," I said.

"Huh? Oh, right. I hear Grandpa sing a line about hope every so often. Like last night, when I was helping him get the campfire going, I heard him singing under his breath . . . let's see, what was that again? Oh yeah, I've got it — 'Strength for today and bright hope for the morrow.' What's up with that?"

"Don't you understand it?"

"Maybe a little."

"You'll understand it better and better as you get older."

"You think so? What makes you say that?"

"Because look how old I am, and I learned something about it just tonight." ◐

One That Didn't Get Away

The screech of the rusty door hinges gave a half-second warning before the darkly confining space around me exploded into light.

"Whoa there, Dad! What're you doing? One of the kids might do that maybe, but you should know enough not to sneak up on somebody in a shanty leaning over a big hole in the ice and yank the door open without some kind of warning. Next time, cough or whistle or hum one of your Lawrence Welkies as you get close. What were you thinking?"

"I made plenty of noise. You mean you didn't hear me?" He stooped slightly and poked his head into the doorway of the biological station's shanty, a weathered wooden structure that my brother Bob and I had set up on the ice on Douglas Lake, about thirty yards offshore of the dorm. "I was practicing my soccer skills with some of those icicle chunks the kids tossed out here yesterday. I got one up in the air and almost nailed the roof of your little shack here."

"I never heard a thing. I was concentrating on what was happening below me in the lake."

"How've you done?" he asked. "Seen anything? Thrown the spear yet?"

"So far I'm zero for zero. But just before you got out here, you should've seen this sucker I've got hooked up. It was in a panic, straining way off under the ice toward the deep water, almost tearing the hook out of its back. It must've seen something coming in, something big and nasty, since it was doing everything it could to get away. That was about as focused as I get. I was so tensed up holding the spear ready that I was starting to feel some burn in my shoulder. Then there you were in the doorway letting practically all the light in the world in here."

"Sorry. Didn't mean to turn any more of your hair gray. I was sure you heard me kicking that loose ice."

"Now that you're out here, you want to come in and watch with me for a while?"

"Cram myself in there?"

"Why not? There are two stools here. I'll snug myself up against the wall. Watching what goes on in the lake is hypnotic."

"I could never squeeze in there," he said. "Not enough space around me. Hardly any light coming in with the door closed. You know I have a little claustrophobia. I don't even like to recall the last time it hit me, that night we had to sleep in that cave-like old bunkhouse on Sugar Island."

"Well, I sure hope you didn't come out here just to scare me and maybe make me miss a fish."

"Nope, I don't walk around out here without a good reason. That would be a prime way to fall and break something. Mom and I are going to make a run into Cheboygan for some groceries, and I was wondering about stopping at Glen's Baits and picking up some more minnows."

"We need more already? This morning we had at least fifteen. What time is it, anyway?"

"Just about two."

"Two? How could we be low on minnows already? Besides the one I've got down this spearing hole, I've got one more on my tip-up. I haven't used any others. Have you and the boys lost that many on your tip-ups?"

"We haven't used them all, but we've gone through a bunch. We've had quite a few flags today — but when we get out here and pull up the line, there's no hooked pike and no minnow left either. I'm not sure why."

"Want to know why?" I said. "Really? Well, then, I'll tell you why. You and your grandsons put out your tip-ups, but then you go and sit in the dorm by the fire playing cards and Yahtzee and whatnot. Then every half hour or so you roll dice to see who has to go out on the deck and use binoculars to check for flags. When a pike takes your minnow and swims off with it, you can't give it all that time. You've got to get out here right away and set the hook. But you guys are all at least a city block away. What's happening is that those pike are grabbing minnows and tripping flags and then ripping your bait off the hook before you guys even notice the flag. And I can't help you out, because the only tip-up I can see out my little peephole is the one I set up — out there toward Pine Point."

"Maybe that's what's going on, but the kids still love rushing out on the lake when they spot a flag. And you should hear all their big talk on the way back to the dorm. It's too much fun to have it stop because we're out of bait. While Mom and I are in town, I'm going to pick up a dozen or two more — maybe a mix of suckers and those emerald shiners."

"It's your money," I said. "But the way you guys are going about things, the only pike you'll ever see from this lake are going to be fish I've speared or caught."

"Brag, brag, brag. I'm still going to come back with some fresh minnows. Where's the bait bucket?"

"Back toward the Lakeside Lab. By that headless snowman the kids made to mark the spot where they spudded out a big hole to keep the bucket in during the day. When you get back, though, check if I'm in here or not. I think I'm going to take a break in a half hour or so. Something's been telling me I didn't have quite enough for lunch. If I'm not out here when you get back, just put the bait bucket in this hole, and when I come out for some more spearing later this afternoon, I'll move the bucket back to where the kids had it. This hole doesn't freeze over during the day."

"Okay. See ya."

I pulled the door shut, scooched my stool up to the edge of the hole, braced a knee against the wall, leaned over cautiously, and focused once more on my hooked sucker, hoping that I wouldn't miss any signs of agitation in the minnow, my cue that it had noticed a cruising pike that had noticed it. After about fifteen minutes, I leaned sideways and brought an eye to my peephole, blinked, tried to focus, blinked again, leaned back and shook my head slightly, found the peephole once more and then, even though no one else was anywhere close enough to hear, yelled, "Flag!"

"Dad and the boys can lose 'em all day long with their dilly-dallying, but not me," I cackled as I squeezed out the door and made for my tip-up, scuff skating in my felt-pack boots on the ice, struggling to zip up my coat while not losing my beanie in the wind. When I reached the tip-up, the spool was still turning: line was peeling off steadily away from the hole, the almost certain sign of a fish. When the spool finally stopped and I grabbed the line to set the hook, I felt the willful resistance of what had to be a good one. I pulled the tip-up out of the hole, rested it on the ice, and started bringing the line in hand over hand.

"Come on, baby, come to Billy. That's it — just keep on swimming right at me. That's it. Oh, so now you want to take some line? Make a little run? Okay, I've got line to give, but you're going to have to work for it. That's enough? You comin' in already? Good, good, come on back this way. You can learn — it'll be a lot easier if you learn to cooperate. Just like that. A little more now, a little more. That's smart. Oh, come on, get serious. What's the point of another run? Turn, come on, turn. This way to the hole. There you go. That's it. Right over here. But I can't get you through the hole sideways. You've got to let me get your head up. I need your snoot first. There, now you'll come. I've got a tool for times like this." With that I gaffed the pike under its jaw and slid it onto the ice, where it threw the hook in a side-flipping frenzy.

It was a decent one, close to thirty inches, with meaty shoulders, definitely worth cleaning for some upcoming meal. But since it was only about the middle of the afternoon, I decided to put the fish on a stringer, attach the stringer to an eyehook screwed into the floor of the shanty, and keep the fish fresh near the surface of the hole that I had been using for spearing. *I'll clean it later, after my break and some more spearing,* I thought, *when I'll probably have a couple more to work on.* I pushed the stools as far back from the hole as I could, leaned the spear against the wall just inside the doorway, and then headed for the dorm.

After I had peeled off most of my cold-weather gear inside, I had a few pieces of fudge, two large almond bars, half a bag of spicy Doritos, and several cups of hot chocolate. Then Jon, Joel, and their cousin Tim tempted me with a version of a rummy game I hadn't played before, and since I never leave a card game until I have won at least one hand, my time in the dorm stretched from what I had expected would be a fairly short break in mid-afternoon until Mom and Dad had returned from Cheboygan, in the mid-winter's early twilight.

Shortly after Dad had eased his truck up along the deck of the dorm, Mom pushed the dorm door open with her foot and came in carrying a large grocery bag with a stalk of celery protruding from its top.

"Boys, don't you think you should see if Grandma needs any help?" My wife, Wanda, was using the voice I remembered from her years as a first-grade teacher.

"Grandma, Grandma," a couple of them called out, "you don't need any help, do you?"

"No, no, I can handle it, but thanks for the offer," she said. "There's only one more bag, and Grandpa's going to bring it in when he comes."

"Where is Dad?" I was trying to see through the dorm's frosted windows and into the truck. "What's taking him so long?"

"Don't you remember?" Mom said. "He bought a pailful of minnows, and he headed out on the ice to put them in the shanty."

"Yikes," I said. "I almost forgot. I was going to do some more spearing after my break, and it's probably too dark for that now. But I've got a fish to clean yet. I better go get it and haul it down to the cleaning table in the Lab."

I laced my boots about halfway up, tossed aside my wool sweater, and pulled on only my down parka. As I followed our pathway through drifts and back onto the lake, now in deep dusk, I heard a strange sound. What was that? Gasping? Wheezing? Choking? Instinctively, I picked up the pace, starting once again to scuff-skate.

"Dad? Dad! Where are you? You out there by the shanty?" I was moving faster than what was safe.

When I got to within eight or ten feet of the shanty, I could see a dark form a step or two to the side of the shanty door. Dad was bent over, hands on his knees, struggling to catch his breath.

"Dad, what's up? You okay? Was the bait bucket too heavy?"

"Naw, naw," he said, but he still wasn't breathing steadily. "I'm fine. And I've got the bait bucket in the hole. Whew! Almost couldn't stop laughing. I can't believe the dumb stuff I do sometimes. Someone should make a movie."

"Dumb stuff? What do you mean? Did you wreck something?"

"Nope. Nothing serious, nothing at all — it's just my own little private joke."

"Tell me."

"Can't. This is a joke that dies with me."

"You're serious?"

"Absolutely. Too embarrassing to tell anyone. So that's that. What brought you out here anyway?"

"I've got to clean my fish, the one on the stringer in the hole."

"Oh, yeah. It's a little dark in there, but that fish looks like a good one. You got it spearing, right?"

"No, got it on my tip-up. It hit just a few minutes after you headed for town."

"With all the time you were spending in the shanty, I thought you might have speared one. Anyway, no matter how you got it, I'm glad you didn't get skunked. But now that I've got some fresh minnows, just wait till tomorrow. The boys and I are going to put you to shame."

"Okay," I said. "When we get out here tomorrow morning, I'll try to look scared. Right now, I've got to go clean that fish."

"You'd better hurry — you don't want to be late for supper."

"This will only take ten minutes or so." I brushed past him into the shanty, groped around until I found the stringer, pulled the pike from the water, unclipped it, dropped it into my five-gallon bucket, and then walked back to the shoreline and followed it to the Lab.

Entering the Lab from the door next to the boat well, I hit the light switch, tossed my parka over a large cylinder, and dumped the pike from the bucket onto the cleaning table. I laid the fish on its side, unsheathed the filet knife that I had left on the table, and ran it through the sharpener a few times. Then, as I was reaching to grasp the fish around its head and hold it secure, I noticed something unusual on its back. Above the rear edge of its gill plate was a hole in its flesh. No, I discovered as I rotated the fish onto its stomach, not one hole but two holes, both of them — it occurred to me as I traced their edges with my index finger — close to the size of a dime. These two holes, many experienced ice anglers would argue, could easily have been made by any one of several tools or pieces of equipment. And they could have been made in any one of several ways, some accidental. And then — it was as if a mental hand flashed out instinctively and enfolded a dragonfly in flight — I understood. I understood what had been so funny. ⑥

PART TWO

Sons and Brothers

Vision

"Uh-oh!"

"Huh? What do you mean, uh-oh?" That was not what I was eager to hear from Wanda as we snuggled in bed that June morning a minute after she had fumbled with the alarm clock and finally hit the snooze bar.

"I think my water just broke."

"That can't be. Your due date is at least three weeks away. You probably just had some strong Braxton-Hicks contractions, and they faked you out. That happens to lots of women in their last month — I've been reading the manuals."

"You can argue all you want, but I think we'll be counting little fingers and toes later today. Braxton Hicks wouldn't lead to this. Look at the bed. Where I was. See?"

She was right, of course. Five hours later she lay sweating but smiling beatifically as she cradled our firstborn, Jonathan Mark, and began comforting him: "Sssh, sssh, sssh. Now, now. There you go. Why you were in such a hurry is a mystery to me. But you had your mind set on June 3, and June 3 it is. We sure had a workout today, didn't we, but we can rest now. See, they're fixing Mama all up. That's it. You don't have to look into that light — it's way too bright. What a miracle you are! Our gorgeous little one of a kind."

But I noticed things that she had missed or had chosen to ignore, things that triggered an acidic clench of concern. As the nurse took Jonathan gently from Wanda and placed him on the scale, his body streaked with a milky fluid, what I noticed first was that his arms and legs looked so fragile that I worried about fractures if we were to lay him down too close to one side or the other of his crib and he were to flail or kick out and hit the railing. Plus, his eyes were gummed up with a substance that he was trying to clear with frantic blinking.

I had always assumed that any baby from the combined genes of Wanda and me would grow rather quickly into someone strong, vigorous, and fully capable of being a regular fishing companion for me. I had imagined someone who could wade upstream on the Flat River with me in the spring, even after thundershowers had turned riffles into boils. Or someone who could stand next to me on the Muskegon in the fall, scan the mosaic of gravel beds extending away from our feet, and confidently point out to me all of those that held spawning king salmon, almost incidentally noting how many males were stacked up behind each female. But the sight of Jonathan's eyes blinking desperately and his wand-like arms and legs jerking spasmodically as he lay on the scale made me wonder.

We'll have to wait and hope, I told myself. But when Jon was released from the hospital, three days later than the four others who had been born on June 3, he did nothing to calm my fears. It seemed that, once he was home, all he wanted to do was sleep.

We had hung above his crib a mobile with several different kinds of fish suspended at various distances above his face. (I had caught Wanda in what was clearly a weak moment and had persuaded her that this mobile would have the greatest cognitive and emotional benefits for our first child.) Right above him, within his reach if he made some effort, were sunfish with flaring orange gill covers, above the sunfish were some smallmouth bass, darkly banded as if they had been taken from stained water, and above them all was a twelve-inch pike with what I saw as a hint of sarcasm on its face. But if Jon ever showed signs of noticing these fish, he did so only when Wanda and I were out of the room.

We had made a couple of cardboard masks — both with big eyes and grinning mouths, one with a sloppy mustache — that we planned to use to play peekaboo with him, hoping that the game would elicit his first definite smiles. But after several episodes of looking like antic fools while he only lost focus and dozed off, we ended up shoving them under his crib and forgetting about them.

With a baby who wanted to sleep almost all the time, what sense did it make for me to unfold the stroller and push him on the asphalt path that started behind Ken-O-Sha School and ran along Plaster Creek? Or what would be the point of taking him down to the Sixth Street Dam, strapping him into a child carrier on my back, and then walking along the river, with most of our time spent watching king salmon thrash their way from one resting pool in the fish ladder up to the next?

His almost constant sleeping made me worry, and I had a hard time keeping my concerns to myself, especially when friends and relatives would stop in to visit and check how he was doing. Once, when my dad and mom came over, I started spiraling through my fears:

"He was born way too early. He's part of the family now, so he should act like it. Wanda and I have been talking for months about all the things we've dreamed about doing with our first child. But he sleeps practically all the time. In fact, it seems that most of the time I'm with him, I'm leaning over his crib with my ear two inches from his nose, straining to hear if he's still breathing. He's got to leave his little dream world behind."

"Are those the only conclusions possible in this neighborhood?" my dad replied. "You don't want to project any clammy stuff onto him, do you? He's probably a child of reflection, of special sight. Seems to me I've read something somewhere about dreaming dreams and seeing visions, and if my memory serves me, those don't come off as negative. So why not let him be? Give him his time and space, and I bet he'll show us a thing or two that no one else can."

"I sure hope you're right. We'll have to compare notes as he gets older. When he makes it to kindergarten or first grade, I'll have to decide whether I dare take him on a little fishing excursion or not, and if I dare, then I'll get a clearer picture of what's going on with him. I just hope that someday he'll be able to focus well enough to catch fish on his own."

I waited until the summer after Jon finished kindergarten, when his immediately younger brother, Joel, had not yet had enough experiences to suspect that his father or mother could ever leave him behind. If Jon could sit in a classroom and draw what he said were dinosaurs and birds, I figured, he should be able to learn how to fool a fish.

Before we set off to some lake or river, I brought Jon into the backyard and started giving him casting lessons. I had bought him a four-foot fiberglass rod with a closed-face casting reel, and on the end of his line I tied a small pyramid-shaped rubber weight. And I must admit that he picked up much of the technique pretty fast. Most people learning to cast have trouble either to the back or the front: they let the weight drop behind them after they take the rod back, or they wait too long after whipping the rod tip forward to hit the release on the reel and smack the area right out in front of them with the weight. Jon was quite skilled to the back and the front; but each time he was about to release the line, he would give his wrist a sudden little twist to the left or the right and send the weighted line sailing sharply to one side or the other. When he snapped his wrist to the left, he came close to putting the weight through the window on the side of our garage. When he snapped it to the right, the weight usually cleared the fence and landed in our neighbor's strawberry beds.

"Straighten it out," I urged. "You can't be so wild when you fish. You've got to remember that, if you had a lure on your line, that lure would have at least one hook on it, and you might be snagging docks and boats and other people. And by 'people' I mainly mean me! I've already got enough scars for two or three people. You don't want to hook your own dad, do you?"

"Why would I want to do that? I'm just trying to put a little extra zing on it when I cast. It's kinda fun seeing where the weight ends up."

"Zing is okay. In fact, zing is great. Once you're actually fishing, you'll cover a lot more water with some zing. On lakes that you've never fished before, you've got to cover the water. But it sure helps to have a good idea of where your lure is going to land."

As much as he practiced, though, he never managed to get the direction of his casts under complete control. I suspected he wasn't really trying. And so his casting had some effect on the details of my plans for our first fishing experience together. I had decided to take him fishing on a visit to the biological station where my brother and his family work and live. That station spreads out along the shoreline of South Fishtail Bay of Douglas Lake. And South Fishtail Bay has a fine-grained sandy bottom extending shallowly for ten or fifteen yards from the shoreline to an extremely sharp drop-off, just off the lip of which the tops of cabbage weeds wave sinuously in the water, especially when the wind is from the southwest.

I had planned to wade in swimsuits and with bare feet, the two of us standing right next to each other, making our way along the drop-off, casting small jigs with yellow twister tails out past the drop-off and retrieving them through the tops of the weeds. If our jigs got hung up in the weeds, we could give our rods a sharp jerk and snap the jigs free. At that point, I knew, fish would often hit. I also knew we could catch just about any kind of fish with those jigs — perch, bluegills, rock bass, smallmouth bass, maybe even a pike or two if they didn't take the jig deep and bite it off. So we were set up for some real action.

But I didn't dare stand too close to him — with his zing on a cast, he might hit me with his rod or come through hard on a bad angle and snag me with his jig. So I revised the plan once we were both in the water, I to the tops of my ankles, he above his knees:

"Jon, I'm going to walk off toward Grapevine Point for thirty yards or so, and then I'll stop and fan cast the water in front of me. Wait a bit, and then you walk and cast your way from here almost to where I am, and when you get fairly close to me, stop casting, slip behind me, walk off thirty yards past, stand there and fan cast, and I'll walk and cast my way up to you. That way we can fish all along the drop-off, and neither of us will be casting to water that the other one already has a lure in. Okay? Good. So you can start right here — but in just a second. Give me time to get out of range. And as you come up to me, don't be sending that jig in my direction. And don't get any closer than this to the edge of the drop-off. Cast out past the edge and reel in quickly. Every so often give the jig some little twitches. If you feel anything, even a little tap, don't hesitate — set the hook. Hard. Almost like you're trying to snap off the tip of your rod. But don't worry — a hard hookset won't break that fiberglass. Okay? We'll talk more when you come up to me."

As I waded away from Jon, I glanced over my shoulder to see how he was doing. He was getting the jig out past the drop-off, though on lots of different angles. And on one of his early casts, maybe his fourth or fifth, his line snapped up taut, his rod bent into a capital C, and a smallmouth bass — better than a foot long — blasted out of the water, shook its head as if crying out to the sun and its attendant clouds about injustice in the universe, and threw the jig.

"Dad, Dad!" Jon yelled. "Did you see that? I mean, did you see that! I had one. I had a fish! It spit the hook out so hard it shot back and almost nailed me in the chest. What kind of fish was that? Will it stick around and bite again?"

"A smallmouth," I said as I turned around and plowed

through the water back toward him. "It's the all-time favorite fish of lots of anglers, and you just saw part of the reason why: they are absolutely wild jumpers. And if you had kept him on longer, you would have discovered more of the reason why people love to catch them: they absolutely refuse to stop fighting. Get them in the net after a ten-minute battle and they're still shaking their head and flaring their fins and flipping around. We better check your drag a second."

His drag was fine, and I moved off once more, grinning. If *hooking a smallmouth doesn't keep him interested*, I thought, *nothing will. Now I'm going to see how well this little guy can focus.*

The fact was, he impressed me. For the next twenty minutes he and I both fished as if we were being filmed for a TV show and had to actually catch some fish, not just point out sandbars and islands on hydrographic maps, demonstrate various knots, brag about fish-attracting scents, and try to sell lures that looked like little underwater helicopters. Not all of Jon's casts were straight out past the drop-off; a few went sideways and landed in only a foot or two of water. But maybe 60 or 70 percent of them landed where he had a chance of hooking another fish. He was so intent that he didn't even notice when I caught and released a hefty rock bass and a not-quite-legal smallmouth.

But then I came up on, almost stumbled on, a surprise. It was again my turn to walk the thirty yards down the shoreline, and as I did so I hit a spread of rocks, some the size of softballs, a few larger, many with sharp-edged chunks cracked off them. The rocks were scattered erratically from the lip of the drop-off all the way back to shore.

"You gotta watch it right in here," I called back to Jon. "There's a whole mess of rocks. You can get through them, but you've got to be super careful. I stepped on one, and it was slippery as snot. Some have edges that can cut you up. Don't step on them, and don't get an ankle wedged between any. Mom's not going to be happy if we have to take you to some emergency room, and I'm not even sure where the nearest one is — probably Cheboygan."

I moved gingerly through the rest of the rocks and down the shoreline, determined not to turn too soon and show Jon that I thought he couldn't navigate the rock field on his own. When I finally turned to look, my mind took a few seconds to make sense of the unexpected image I saw. Jon had reeled his jig all the way to his rod tip, and he was down on both knees in the shallow water, hunched over, probing in the water before him with his rod.

"What are you doing?" I yelled. "That's probably the best way in the world to snap off the tip of your rod. You don't want to break it the first day on a lake, do you? That would be a lousy record. You'd have to find some extra chores around the house to buy a new one."

"Dad, you gotta come over here and see these. There's a bunch of little lobsters all around here. About two inches long. It's just like in the book Mrs. De Jong read to us in school — about an island boy on the Atlantic shore catching lobsters in tide pools. Whoa! They go backwards. Dad, come here! Come here! You gotta see them all. They're all over the place. I think every rock has a little lobster under it."

"Well, don't just look at them. See if you can catch some. Those little pinchers can't hurt that much. If their shell is soft, they make great smallmouth bait. They'd probably attract smallmouth all the way from the other side of the bay."

"Bait? These little babies are mad cool, way too cool to use for bait. I've got to check them out for a while."

"Jon, they're just crayfish. Seen one, seen 'em all. We've got to get back at it — we've got plenty of shoreline to fish yet. I was hoping to make it all the way down to that little cove just this side of Grapevine. Okay, Jon? Jon!"

But he didn't look up. And I knew that our fishing excursion was over. I had lost him to a bunch of freshwater crustaceans. I waded toward shore, found a blown-over popple lying almost parallel to the shoreline, used it as a backrest, and watched Jon poking among the rocks, so excited that he was making snorty little noises to himself.

To be fair to him, I thought, I'd have to say that he did great until he discovered those crayfish. And I think he was enjoying himself almost as much as I was as we fished our way along the drop-off. I guess I'll have to give him a few tries in the boat. There's just too much stuff to distract him when he's wading.

A few weeks later I started buckling him into a lifejacket and taking him out in the boat with me. But he always seemed as interested in peering over the side of the boat as he was in casting for fish. He'd marvel at the translucent weeds near the boat launch on Miner Lake, billowing greenish masses that made me think of a cotton-candy machine gone out of control. He'd use the handle of the net to probe among the water lilies growing around the mouth of the small channel running north out of Wabasis Lake, once uncovering a pair of turtles in what looked to me like coital embrace ("What were they doing, Dad — wrestling?"). And whenever I'd use the trolling motor to take us humming into some quiet bay, he'd put his rod down, lean over the gunnel, and look for minnows or surface striders or water beetles or snakes. No matter what kind of creature it was, if it moved in the water, shallow or deep, Jon was always the first to spot it.

At some point that summer, Jon discovered that I usually kept a small disposable camera — I'd buy it with a coupon for $5.95, use its twenty-four exposures, and turn the whole thing in for developing — tucked in one of the pockets of my tackle bag. I had learned that I was going to need pictures of the big fish I caught, since the person closest to me in all the world had the hardest time believing what I told her about my angling prowess.

"A likely story," Wanda would say. "A twenty-four-inch bass out of that little lake? We drive by it all the time on the way to the Schmidts' place, and nothing about it would ever lead anyone to think it could hold a twenty-four-inch bass. A bunch of minnows maybe. What would a fish like that have to weigh? Seven or eight pounds? You got a picture? Start showing me pictures and I'll start believing your stories. Evidence. That's the key. Anybody who knows anything about you knows you tell the truth only about sixty-five percent of the time. And some of that sixty-five percent is actually exaggeration. You don't have to give me that look — you know I'm right. So show me some pictures."

As Jon and I extended the range of our fishing trips that summer, more and more often he would put down his rod, find my little camera, and ask me to hold the boat as steady as possible while he focused on something in, on, or around the lake we were exploring.

"Make sure you keep track," I'd warn him. "You've got to save at least one exposure. What happens when I catch the fish of my lifetime and we don't have any film left? Huh? You know what Mom says about pictures. So save at least one shot. Probably you should save two or three. If I catch a monster fish, I'd want pictures from more than one angle. I paid for the camera, you know."

He didn't always remember, but he avoided any serious trouble with me because I never caught anything that summer that I would be tempted to call the fish of my lifetime. And as the summer wore on, he started showing that he was not using my camera in ways that everyone would regard as worthless. Pictures began to appear on the walls of our family room, pictures that were attractively matted (Jon had enlisted the aid of his mother's considerable memory-book skills) and inserted in oak frames that the two of them had found at our local variety store.

One of his photographs looked very much like an impressionist painting: it showed small yellow and green spots splashed across a darkly reflective, almost metallic, background. Looking at it really closely, though, you would realize that some of the spots were slightly larger and more irregular in shape than the others and that these spots marked the body of a leopard frog sitting in a mass of duckweed.

From a little distance, another of his photographs looked like one that should have been discarded, the product of someone's handling the camera clumsily and pressing the shutter by mistake, but all it apparently showed was a section of a fishing rod — a section quite close to but not including the tip — running from the lower left to the upper right corner of the photo.

But the merest hint of gossamer extending on each side of the rod revealed the truth: resting between two line guides, the hue of its body an almost perfect match for the crimson of the rod, was a damselfly so delicate that it must have escaped straight from a poet's dream.

For the rest of that summer, whenever Jon would look around himself and notice something that he wanted a picture of, he seemed to remember what I wanted him to remember: that we were, after all, out on the water not to hone skills in composing a visual image and holding a disposable camera steady but to try to catch fish. He knew, I think, that I was often watching him over my shoulder, and he was smart enough to make his times of photographic experimentation sporadic and brief.

Therefore, he never broke the implicit anglers' code that holds whenever two or more are gathered together to fish: the code does not forbid certain activities, such as snack breaks, but it does hold that all those in a fishing party make an effort to keep their lures in the water as consistently as possible. The more consistently lures are kept in the water, the more chances for fish to strike; the more chances for fish to strike, the greater the number of fish likely to be landed; the greater the number of fish landed, the more often the anglers can engage in celebratory practices that they rarely have a chance for in their lives off the water. And the more often the anglers can engage in such practices, the less likely it will be for any corrosive questions about their essential skill as anglers to work their way into their minds.

On our very first excursion the next summer, however, Jon started to break the code. What he would do was reel his line up, balance his rod against a storage compartment so that its tip extended over the side of the boat, lean back on his seat, cross his arms over his chest, and stare — just stare — into the distance, adjusting his apparent focal point only slightly and occasionally. There he would be, sitting in something like a trance for five or six minutes.

After the first one of these that I ever noticed, I asked him, "What were you doing? You getting a headache or something? We've been waiting since last summer to get back out here, you know. At least I have been. And you said you were. So here we finally are, out on the water again, and you're just sitting and staring into space. What's up with that?"

"I want to make sure I don't miss anything."

"Miss anything? Whataya mean? The only thing you're going to miss is a fish. Maybe a big one."

"Don't worry, Dad, I'll still catch my share. Maybe even more than my share."

"I'd like to know how. What are they supposed to do, jump out of the water to get to your lure? I have yet to meet a suicidal fish."

But the eerie thing was that he was right. After staring at what I could only guess was a bird in a bush or a dog on a dock, he might aim my camera, exhale slowly, and press the shutter. Or he might not. In either case, he would then pick up his rod, make a nonchalant cast off one side of the boat or the other, and frequently catch a fish. It was uncanny: some steady and quiet focusing into the distance, maybe a picture, a seemingly aimless cast, and then, shockingly, often a wild fight with a fish.

❦

As long as he was catching fish after so many of his spells, I decided that I would have to accept his strange rhythm of activity when he and I spent time together in the boat. But I struggled with the question of whether I dared take Jon along when my adult fishing partner, Duzzer, and I would set aside a day for offering some higher education to the fish in a West Michigan lake. What would Duzzer think of someone who spent nearly as much time staring across the water as he did reeling a lure through it? But finally one day, near the end of the second summer that Jon and I fished together, I went ahead and took the chance, and on that day Jon ended up catching one of the bigger fish I have ever seen anyone catch in Michigan.

We were on Muskegon Lake on a humid evening in late August. As the light over the dunes went pink, Jon roused himself from one of his meditations, stood up, and cast an orange Mepps spinner toward the mouth of the Muskegon River. Two seconds later, giving a little grunt, he set the hook on a fish.

"What is it?" I shouted. "A good one?"

"I don't know for sure. It could be. It hit like a rhino, but now it's hard to tell. I think it's swimming at the boat. Look at my line, it's slicing toward us. Here it comes — what's this fish going to do, ram the boat?"

Jon continued to take up line as fast as he could, and a few seconds later Duzzer spotted the fish: "It's a big fish! A huge fish! I'm not kidding. I don't know what it is, but it's the biggest fish I've ever seen north of Gulf Shores. It's a big fish! Are you kidding me — it's enormous!"

"Fight him, Jon, fight him!" I started a running pep talk.

"Tire him out. Let him take some drag if you need to. That's it, that's it, let him make all the runs he wants. You don't have to worry about snags — we're out in pretty deep water and drifting into deeper. You'll get him, you'll get him. Just be patient. You can't horse him. He'll come when he's pooped. You checked your drag, right? Yup. Yup. You're wearing him down. I think you're going to get him. Just tire him out. Let him fight the rod and the drag. Here he is, right up here, out in front of me just a bit. My goodness gracious — he's a monster!"

As I said that, the fish dove and ran under the bow. Jon dipped the tip of his rod deep into the water, brushed past me, made sure his line passed under the trolling motor propeller, and then gained a little line as the fish paused in its run away from the other side of the boat.

"My fingers! I can't straighten out my fingers. It feels like I'm hooked into a horse."

"You want me to take the rod for a few seconds?" I asked, moving next to Jon.

"No, no, no. This is my fish. I can fight him. Where's the net? Is the net ready? I've got him turned back toward us. Maybe I can start pumping him up to the side of the boat. Come on. That's it. Just a little bit more. Get your head up here. Just let me lift your chin. Come on, fishie."

"Oh my, oh my, oh my," Duzzer cried, his voice going falsetto. "It's gigantuan! I'm not sure we can get it in the net! And if we do, we might not want it in the boat with us — if it thrashes, it could break our legs!"

"Maybe one of those pike who spend part of the year having all those easy alewife meals out in Lake Michigan," I said.

"It's no pike," Duzzer replied, "and no walleye either — too fat for both. Especially up by its head. The back of its head is huge, six or seven inches across. Maybe it's a sturgeon — saw one of those on the news this spring. I don't know what it is for sure, but we're getting close. Can you bring it in a few more feet, Jon? It looks like it might start wallowing on the surface."

"Ungh, yeah, maybe. I'm trying. There. How's that? Can you get it?"

"I think so. Maybe. Here we go." And with that, Duzzer made a decisive swoop with the net, waggled the rim of the net vigorously to get the tail of the fish down into the cords, started to lift the fish, lurched over sideways toward the stern, got his feet back under himself, and then hauled the fish over the side, the net handle cracking in the process.

"It's a catfish!" Jon shouted. "A monster catfish."

And he was right. If we had been fishing somewhere down along the Mississippi River, we probably would not have gotten so excited about a channel cat this size. But for us, never having intentionally tried for catfish, having a fish nearly four feet long and over forty pounds in the boat with us was more than enough to make Duzzer and me start chanting, "Wild thing, I think I love you!" — loud enough to scare people out of their after-dinner reveries on their decks in North Muskegon.

"We are some fine fishermen, if I do say so myself. We are some fine fisherman!" Duzzer crowed.

"Absolutely," I agreed as I used a heavy pliers to twist the hook out of the corner of the fish's mouth. "Guess what, Jon? This could be the fish of your lifetime. It would be the fish of my lifetime, that's for sure. Let's see, I'm not even sure how you're supposed to hold a catfish up for a picture. I guess we should try a couple of shots holding the fish horizontally and then a couple with the top of its head and its back toward the camera. I'm pretty sure I've seen pictures in magazines of people holding catfish that way. Jon, you ease around here, and I'll help you hold the fish up. It's almost as long as you are, it really is. Find the camera and give it to Duzzer."

"Dad," Jon whispered, his eyes to the side, "I know what you're always saying about saving a picture or two, but back when we were up in the shallows in Snug Harbor, a swan with a bunch of different grays and whites in its wings started swimming around the boat, and I lost track of all the pictures I was snapping. I guess I already used them all up."

"Are you kidding me? You used up all the film? On a swan? This is the biggest fish I've ever had in the boat, and we're not going to get even one picture of it? Wait a minute — Duzzer, do you have a camera along?"

"Not here. Mine stays in a compartment in my own boat."

"Oh, my goodness gracious alive. Who knows when we'll catch anything close to this again? Jon, please — please just check the camera again. Maybe you figured wrong and there's a shot left."

"I'm not joking, Dad. I wish I was, but I'm not. I used up the last four pictures on that swan. It was so close I could almost touch it with my rod. When am I going to have a chance to get close enough to get pictures like that again?"

"Close to a swan? What's the big deal? Take a walk around Reeds Lake, and you can get close to a swan. Or sit on the beach at Wabasis and get close to a whole family of swans — father, mother, baby, baby, baby, baby! The big deal is, the really big deal is, when are you gonna have a chance to get a picture of a fish like this again? This is probably a once-in-a-lifetime. I've got to sit down. I can't believe this is happening. Whew! Wait a minute. Maybe we could put this fish in the livewell and then head over to that bait shop by the state park and show them what we've caught. They must have a camera there. Probably a Polaroid. People must bring fish in there all the time to show off."

"Bill," Duzzer said, sounding emphatic, "a fish like this is never going to fit in the livewell. Nobody builds livewells for a fish like this."

"Dad," Jon said, "I don't want my fish to die. It's going to die if we don't get it back in the water. It can't die." He was close to whimpering.

"Okay, we don't have a choice. No choice, I guess. Let's get it back in the water. It weighs a ton. What a shame! There. Hold it by the tail. There you go. That's it. And you can twist it side to side just a bit to help it get its bearings. There, I think it's ready, Jon. Let it go and see if it's ready. There it goes. See it? It's still in good shape. I hope your mother will believe you about this, because she sure won't believe me."

"But I've got a good picture of it," Jon said.

"Not in the mood for jokes, Jon."

"I'm not joking. I do have a good picture. And I'm not going to lose it. It's right here — in my head."

Later, after we had trailered the boat and while we were waiting for Jon to get up from the end of a nearby dock, where he had gone down on his stomach to feed bits of potato chips to mallards, I turned to Duzzer.

"So what do you think? Do you mind having him along? It's not like he fishes nearly as steadily as you and I do. It can get a little annoying, I know. I guess I've just learned to live with it when we've gone out. But he doesn't have to come along any more when you and I have a day on the water."

"Are you kidding?" Duzzer said. "Who cares that he doesn't fish all the time? Let him take all the breaks and pictures he feels like. You saw what happened today. Just about every time he made a cast after sitting there, he caught a fish. And then he topped the whole day off by catching practically the biggest fish you and I have ever been around. It's like a magic show. As far as I'm concerned, he can come with us whenever he wants to — your boat, my boat, standing on shore, or wading in rivers. If I were you, though, I'd make sure that somehow he gets his own camera. As much as that kid loves taking pictures, he should have a camera of his own. Then he could shoot away, and you'd always have your camera in your tackle box — with plenty of film."

I was sure that Jon was too far away to hear that comment, but by the time he and I ventured out again two weeks later, he had found a way to earn and save enough money to buy a disposable camera, which he kept in a Ziploc bag in his own plastic tackle box. And at some point after that trip, his behavior around the house was transformed: instead of trying to invent clever reasons why he could not help me rake up the sycamore leaves in the backyard or trim the shrubs in the front, he became almost annoyingly insistent with his questions about errands in and around the house and about how much they were worth.

"Jon," I said at one point, "it's great that you want to help Mom and me so much, but do you think it's right to ask us to pay you for everything you do, like putting the toothpaste cap back on after you use it?"

"You don't have to pay me for everything, Dad, but I can use all the work and money you can find for me. I'm saving everything I make for a digital camera. I can do some things with those disposable cameras, but with a digital you won't believe the pictures I'll be able to take."

The persistence of a young boy with one clear thing on his mind can be unnerving. By the next summer, Jon had saved enough to buy himself a respectable digital camera. And in the four or five years after that, he kept saving, all in an effort to add to his equipment — additional lenses first, special filters later. All of the new equipment never changed his pattern of activity in the boat — with me at first and then with his two younger brothers and me later on. He continued to put his rod down from time to time, stare across the water for five or six minutes, perhaps take up his camera and shoot, then make a random cast, and frequently end up fighting another fish.

What did change was the quality of his photos. From the start he had done impressive work with the disposable, but with his digital equipment he was leading me to enlarge and even revise my view of the natural world. For the first time in my life, I saw that loons do not have a bill like, say, a mallard's, but instead brandished a living dagger. And when I focused closely on one of Jon's images of a male wood duck, I had to fight off the thought that the hue of those irises was impossible.

Another thing that changed once Jon started bringing good camera equipment into the boat concerned the extra care we all had to start taking. Imagine lurching around while trying to halt the powerful run of a pike away from the boat, pulling back on your rod hard and then harder, arching your back against the fish's strength and desperation, and then when the fish turns, losing your balance so that you trip and smash one of the lenses with your knee. Or imagine trying to unhook a big pike as it ties itself up in the net in the bottom of the boat, untangling the mess, subduing the fish, forcing its jaws open, probing with a pliers until you can get a hold of the treble hook and can twist it out of cartilage, lifting the fish free of the net, and then watching it flip from your hands and thrash in the bottom of the boat, threatening to leave a thick coating of pike slime all over a camera. Jon learned quite quickly, then, that he had to keep his camera and lenses as far as possible from us and any boated fish; Joel, Jason, and I learned to fish with a divided consciousness, part of our mind on our casting and fighting and unhooking, part on the location of Jon's camera and lenses.

We can live like this, I often thought in those days. *I think we can live like this. We need to take quite a bit more care than anglers usually do, and every once in a while that seems like a hassle, but at least the four of us can keep getting out together in the same boat. With more experience, the Vande Kopple & Sons Angling Enterprise is only going to become more and more skilled, maybe even formidable.*

In the next period of the family's fishing history, my predictions and hopes were fulfilled. Jon, Joel, Jason, and I pulled the boat to lake after lake throughout West Michigan — from Pine Lake in the south to Lincoln in the north, from Muskegon Lake in the west to Morrison in the east. And no matter how different any one of these lakes was from those we had fished before, within an hour or two of being on it, we would usually do a respectable job of figuring out what kind of fish it held, where they were hiding, and how we should go about trying to fool them. And Jon kept adding to his collection of photographs.

As the boys grew into their teens, I kept a promise I had made to them when they were quite young. I started taking the three of them, along with a friend or two, to some fishing camp in Ontario for a week each summer. But in the late spring prior to our second trip to Eagle Lake, I had to confront once more the fear that I had worked to subdue ever since the time when Jon shifted his focus from smallmouth bass to crayfish. This fear began to throb anew with a simple question from Jon, who was now almost fifteen: "Dad, we're going to Eagle again this summer, right?"

"Right. Everything's set. Six guys this trip — you, Joel, Jason, Duzzer, T-Gunz, and me. We're in number two, the cabin you guys like so well, the same cabin we were in last summer."

"So I was thinking . . ."

"Yeah?"

"I was thinking — well, you know how much I love taking pictures of stuff around lakes, right?"

"Anyone who's ever been within a hundred yards of our boat knows you love taking pictures."

"Yeah, well, I was wondering if this time around I could try something a little different. I'll pay for it myself. You wouldn't have to pay anything extra. I've already got the money saved up."

"What is it? What are you saving up for?"

"Well, do you think . . . just listen to me first . . . do you think I could rent my own boat? That way, I could go wherever I thought the best pictures would be and I could take as much time getting set up as I wanted, and I wouldn't have to hold you guys up at all, and I wouldn't have camera equipment in anybody's way. Plus, I wouldn't need one of those expensive Alaskan upgrade boats. Just a regular fourteen-foot aluminum with a fifteen or twenty-five horse. I've already checked the price list on the Net, and it's not too bad. Please, Dad. Dad?"

"My goodness."

"What?"

"I don't even know where to start."

"Just say it's okay, please, Dad. Just say it's okay. Since I came up with this idea a month or so ago, I've been so excited it's been hard to get to sleep at night. I just keep imagining all the different stuff I could check out."

"But Jon, you're forgetting that this is a fishing trip. The reason we travel eighteen hours to northwest Ontario is to catch fish. At Eagle you can fish for all kinds of fish. And you can catch a trophy of any one of them. I've even heard that Eagle Lake had the world-record musky for a while. We don't burn all that gas just to go north and take pictures."

"But I'll fish. I never just take pictures. You know that. I look around and then sometimes I shoot, and then I make a cast. And you know when I make a cast I almost always catch a fish. You've seen that."

"I have never understood it," I said. "But you're right. You often end up catching more and bigger fish than the rest of us do. But we go on these trips to have experiences and make memories together. You know that most of my best memories of you boys come from our times on the water. When I'm old and my arthritis makes it too painful to walk, I want to remember as many times as possible in the boat with all three of you. I really don't like the idea of you being off by yourself all day long."

"But Dad, look at what happens on these trips. The four of us never go out in one boat together. We always divide up. You and Duzzer like to fish together a lot, and sometimes one of us kids goes along with you. But I can't remember the last trip when you fished with us three boys in one boat. Plus, I won't be off by myself for the whole time. We'll all be together for card games once it gets dark. And each night I can show everybody pictures of where I've been and what I've seen. I can even hook my camera up to T-Gunz's laptop, you know, and that way everybody gets to have more experiences. The more experiences for everyone, the more memories. Please, Dad, this would be perfect for me."

"But you know how I worry about you boys, even when I can see all of our boats spread out around the same bay. What if you were gone somewhere by yourself and got hurt? Have you forgotten that time Jason got that big hook practically all the way through his thumb? When I first saw him hunched over in that boat, he was almost in shock. Don't you remember how white he was? Or how about the time I was trying to help you unhook that pike and it ended up slashing a couple of my fingers? Huh? Have you forgotten about stuff like that? If I hadn't been able to wrap up those fingers with duct tape, I would have been in some serious trouble. And what's going to keep you from getting lost? In most sections Eagle is a maze, a big glistening maze. Half the time when I'm driving the boat I'm wondering, *Where's the channel? Is that the channel? What happened to that buoy we saw on the way down? What's that over there — an island or a peninsula off the* mainland? *Where is that point with the eagles' nest?* If I let you go out by yourself, I'll be a nervous wreck the whole week. Do you ever think what it's like to be a dad? Have you thought what it would be like for me to have to stand on the dock at dusk, straining to hear if a boat is coming back into our bay?"

"Do you ever think what it's like to be a kid? I can do stuff. You worry enough for three or four people. You know that, right?"

"It's not all worry. A lot is just being careful and prepared. But I know I can worry."

"And you know I'm a careful kid. When have you ever seen me take a big risk? I promise to be as careful on Eagle Lake as I've always been everywhere else. I took that special course in eighth grade to get my boater's permit, remember? And I won't get lost. I know I won't get lost. I learned most areas of Vermillion Bay last summer. And I'll never go anywhere new unless I'm sure I can find my way back — bit by bit with the map. Not too long from now I take my driver's test, and after that I'll have to find my way all over the place. You've got to let me get started on my own, Dad. Danny — you know Danny, the lodge owner's son — is younger than I am, and he flies all around Eagle Lake by himself. He had to get started sometime. And Mike — you know the musky guide — Mike told me he started guiding when he was just a kid. Please, Dad. Please let me try this."

"This is no small deal, Jon. This is plenty scary for me. I'll have to think about it. I wonder what Mom will say."

"She thinks it's okay. I already checked. She knows I'll be really careful. And she knows that this is something I would absolutely love to do."

"All right. All right. Give me a couple of days, and I'll give you an answer."

But I'm sure that he knew what the answer would be. As we had gone back and forth, I had conceded a point or two. I had never uttered an absolute "no." And I believed him when he said that he had Wanda's permission. So I had to resign myself to imagining him loading his gear into his own rented boat, pushing off from the dock, and then cutting through the chop so common on Vermillion Bay toward something notable he suspected lay in the distance.

Jon had been right about how we divided up when we fished Eagle. For a couple of days Duzzer and I were together in one boat, while Joel, Jason, and T-Gunz were in another. We usually stayed within sight of each other. On Tuesday, Jason joined Duzzer and me; on Wednesday, Joel took a turn. Both of them said they needed to figure out what it was that Duzzer and I were doing to keep our numbers of fish landed so much lower than theirs. On Thursday, T-Gunz fished with Duzzer and me, not really to observe and correct — he didn't have quite enough fishing experience for that — but mainly to talk with Duzzer about what it was like to coach high-school sports.

During those days, I didn't have Jon's boat in sight all the time. Occasionally we would backtroll across the mouth of a bay and I would glance to the side and see him floating way up in the back of the bay, almost hidden in the wild rice. And once, while Duzzer and I were returning from a foray to Railroad Bay, I happened to glance over to the south shore of Strawberry Island and noticed Jon's boat nosed up between cedars blown down along a rocky point.

It wasn't until after dark, when we all were back in the cabin and some of the boys were starting to brag, that we found out exactly what Jon had been focusing on each day. He would hook up his camera to the laptop, and we would huddle around him and ask, "What is that? Is that a mink? How did you ever spot it in all those rocks? How did you get so close?" Or "What kind of bird is that? It looks like it has some kind of crown." Or "How in the world did you ever notice that that loon was swimming along with a baby on its back? Didn't the baby seem scared?"

At some point, Joel or Jason or T-Gunz would ask, "How about fish? We did pretty well today. Did you catch anything?"

"Oh, I've got pictures of fish," he would respond, calmly and confidently. And then he would start to scroll through pictures of impressive fish, all of which he made sure I saw: fat smallmouth lying in the bottom of the boat with their tail at one end of a measuring tape and their lips brushing up against the line marking twenty-two inches; a couple of fat pike with spinnerbaits still in the corner of their mouths; pike lying almost over on their side among pencil reeds in shallow water; and a fine musky — probably forty-four or forty-five inches long — that Jon, prior to releasing it, had managed to hold by the tail in the water with his left hand and photograph with his right.

His nightly slide shows helped me start to relax. But I couldn't quite break myself of the habit of reminding him each day that he shouldn't motor off too far from camp. And whenever I was on the water, even when exploring a weedbed so vast that it promised to hold more than one hog musky, I would scan the water, near and far, hoping to catch a glimpse of Jon.

∞

On Friday, our last day on Eagle, I decided to share a boat with Joel and Jason, even though their way on the water was not my favorite. As young as they were, for them fishing had become an almost obsessive hunt for trophies. And not trophies of any species — just muskies. They had spent quite a bit of time up in the main lodge listening to the tales of the lodge owner, Hubie, and some of the guides about monster muskies, fish that not even the best of them had been able to fool and subdue.

One story was about a musky known to patrol Coleman's reef. According to a guide who often took clients to the reef, one time this fish had appeared out of the dark just to the side of a gull, and before the gull managed to flap and peck and scream its way out of danger, the fish grabbed the frantic bird by one of its wings and took it under, leaving only a couple of feathers on the surface.

Probably the most famous story of all was about an angler from Chicago who was being guided down in the central part of the lake by Mike, one of the long-time guides. The client had cast out a Suick in Meridian Bay and then turned to rummage in his rucksack for a granola bar.

"Set the hook! Now, now, now! Set the hook hard!" Mike screamed, for he had seen a monster musky, fifty-six inches or so, rush the Suick from the side and clamp down on it. The client dropped the granola bar, went into a sweeping hookset, and fought that fish hard for twenty or twenty-five minutes.

"It could have been the biggest musky I've ever seen on Eagle," Mike said, "and I've been guiding here for twenty-two years. If a fish like that ever shows itself to you and you're not expecting it, you're probably going to need a defibrillator." Finally, the client managed to work that musky to within six or seven feet of the stern of the boat, just out of Mike's reach with the net, when the fish went into yet another head-shaking frenzy and the hook that was in the corner of its mouth, Mike said, just "pulled free." The musky lay just below the surface for a second and then flicked its tail and dove.

It was only about one o'clock. So Mike and his client could have fished for at least three more hours. And it was only the Wednesday of a full week that the man had booked. But after sitting quietly in the boat for ten or twelve minutes, taking small bites of his granola bar and chewing very thoroughly, the man asked to be motored back to camp. There he gathered up all his fishing gear from the boat and plodded up to his cabin, packed his Suburban very methodically, walked over to the office and paid for the entire week without saying a word about what had happened, climbed behind the wheel of his vehicle, stared out over the water for a few minutes, and then started up and left for home.

Some people I know would call these stories the exaggerated fantasies of guides who spend too many hours in the sun each summer and then each winter lie around in a near-frigid mobile home resting somewhat unevenly on cinder blocks. And some mortals might even have gotten up halfway through one of the tales and left, muttering under their breath about never before being asked to accept a bigger collection of lies. But Joel and Jason took all these stories as the words of significant truth, words that directed them to their core mission at that point in their lives.

So they became little Ahabs in their pursuit of monster

muskies. This meant that they would fish only those spots that, with a guide or on their own, they had discovered held big fish. It meant that they spent only enough time on a spot to learn whether any fish were moving — six or eight casts each through a medium-sized weedbed. If no fish showed itself, they would reel up and roar off to another spot. And it meant that they often seemed fully satisfied to spend twelve or fourteen hours on the water and come back to the cabin and report that they had had follows from two big fish that day.

"Follows!" Duzzer would snort. "You mean you spent the whole day out there and you didn't hook a thing? What good are a couple of follows? If all we wanted to do was see fish, we'd drive to Chicago and visit the Shedd Aquarium!"

"Follows are good," they would respond, something close to reverence in their tones. "Follows are very good. Those fish showed themselves to us. Now we know where they are."

My favorite kind of fishing was less hurried and more varied. Most of all, I wanted to be fighting a fish every fifteen minutes or so, to feel life on the end of the line. So I would try some of the same spots that Joel and Jason tried for musky. But if I didn't see a fish in six or eight of these spots, then I might motor up into a shallow bay and buzz spinnerbaits through pencil reeds for pike. I can't deny that some of these would be what many people dismiss as "hammerhandles," but they almost always hit harder than their size would suggest, and it was a challenge to land them since they all apparently knew from birth how to take fishing line down and around the base of reeds. Or I might tie on a suspending minnow bait and twitch it over and around rust-colored reefs, irritating the smallmouth again and again, just irritating them until they couldn't keep themselves from biting. In any case, I knew very well that if I went out for the day with Joel and Jason, I would have to be ready to fly from one potential big-fish spot to another with them. But I wanted to spend the last full day in a boat with as many of my sons as possible.

The first spot we tried was the rocky saddle between Musky Point and two buoys roughly fifty yards offshore. Joel was working a Cowgirl just below the surface, Jason was giving a shallow-running Burt erratic twitches, and I followed up with a magnum Bomber minnow that I was banging through boulders. About ten casts each. No strikes. No slashes at our baits. No boils. No follows. So we stowed our rods and motored off to a large weedbed southeast of Sunset Island.

I decided to switch lures, to snap on something that could work through the weeds better than a Bomber. *Time for a Suick*, I thought. While working to get the snap of my leader through the eye of the lure, I looked up when I heard Joel sucking breath through his teeth.

"A follow. Look. It's a big one, a really big one. It's hot, right on my spinner. Ach, it nipped. It nipped the skirt, but it didn't get the hook. Here we go, here we go — a nice smooth L-turn. Maybe I can set her off. Eat it, baby! How about a snack with a little surprise in it? Ah, shoot, I think she saw the boat. She's gone, under the boat and out of sight."

"Too bad," Jason said, laughing. "We would have had a double. Look what I've got." And he nodded at some light splashing in the distance. "It's just a little snot — a skinny pike. About twenty-two inches. Not much fight against this tackle. It's probably going to be a twirler."

As he said that, the pike started to roll on its side, and when it did, an enormous musky — was it the one Joel called up? —

appeared and smacked that pike in the side so hard that it folded into a U and flew a couple of feet into the air. Before the pike hit the surface, the musky propelled itself after it and clamped down on it sideways behind the gills. And when the musky landed, it stirred up a frothing storm in the water by shaking the pike, apparently trying to tear it in half.

"Dad, Dad, get the camera!" Jason couldn't hide the quaver in his voice. "We've heard stories about musky attacks, but we've never seen any. You've got to get some pictures! Look at that monster rip up the pike!"

I grabbed the camera, moved up on Jason's shoulder, centered the fish in the viewfinder, reminded myself to keep my fingers out of the way, and started shooting as fast as I could hit the rewind wheel.

"Look, look," Joel said, now at my side. "It must have heard us or something. It let go of the pike and swam off toward the island. Can you believe it? That was like a grenade in the water."

"That pike is a mess," I said. "Look at those flaps of bloody flesh. Reel up, Jase, and we'll unhook what's left of the pike."

But Jason was bent over, his free hand on his left knee, his breathing heavy.

"Want me to do it?" I offered. "I'll reel while you catch your breath."

"I'll . . . I'll get it," Jason said, swinging his rod away from me. "It felt like . . . you can't believe it . . . it felt like the top of my head was going to blow off there for a second. Still a little lightheaded. Whew! I'll reel up."

As soon as Jason put some pressure on the torn-up pike and brought it toward us, its body quivered, a very weak death spasm, and the musky appeared again. This time it was on the other side of the pike, and its mouth clamped down sideways over the pike's entire head.

"Wh — ! This is unbelievable! That thing is a brute!" Jason yelled, and he was panting again.

"Can you get them closer, Jase?" I said. "I'll get even better pictures. They'll be fantastic. Joel, get the net ready. If Jase can bring them in just a bit more, we'll get both the musky and the pike in the net, at least what's left of the pike. Can you bring them toward us? That's probably our biggest musky ever."

"There," Jason said, putting his back into it. "That's a couple of feet. I think I can gain a little bit more. That musky is mainly sideways in the water — it's like pulling on a semi tire."

"Great," I said. "There — I've got another few shots. Joel, you ready with the net? Remember, wait till you can get the musky by the head — don't worry about the pike."

"I know how to net fish — one fish, two fish, it doesn't matter!"

"Cool it, cool it. It's just that netting an unhooked fish would make a fabulous story. We'll tell people, and they'll say we're the biggest storytellers on the lake."

"I'll get it," Joel said. "Just watch. A little more toward me, Jase, and we'll have him."

But just then something — whether noise from our boat or changed pressure on the line or whatever — apparently alarmed the musky and it opened its jaws, released the mangled pike, waggled its head, swam under the bow, and was gone.

"No! No! No! No!" Jason shouted, kicking the side of the boat.

I tried to stop him with words: "Whoa, whoa. Easy, Jase! Putting your boot through the boat is not going to help anything. I've heard more than a few stories of muskies attacking hooked fish. And you know what? I don't very often hear of anyone getting the musky into the net. And I'm sure I got some good pictures of that beast, especially the second time around. You brought him in here really close. I bet I took over a dozen pictures — I was going hot and heavy there. Some of those are sure to turn out great."

"Yeah," Joel said, sensing that I needed some help, "and that was only the second spot of the day. We've got more spots to try than we'll have time for — Flattop Reef next, then Little Flattop, then down around Biblecamp Point. We'll get fish — you know we'll get some. Plus what's the big deal about netting a fish that none of us even had a hook in? Just take a deep breath and calm down. From what we've seen so far, it looks like the hogs are moving today."

Most of what Joel said was right. But he was wrong about the activity level of the fish. After the attack near Sunset, we fished hard for over three hours, and not one of us had even a lazy follow. Finally, I had had enough of an eight-foot heavy-action rod, eighty-pound-test line, and lures up to a foot long.

"I'm switching," I told the boys as I reached for my medium-action rod and started to tie on a three-inch suspend-ing Rebel minnow. "If no musky is going to pay us any atten-tion, then I'm going to catch some smallmouth. So many of the spots we're fishing have rock beds and ledges, and you know there's got to be smallmouth around them. I can't keep casting for muskies. If the muscles in my neck and shoulders get any tighter, they'll pull right off the bone."

"Pretty risky, don't you think?" Joel chided. "What pound test you got on that little reel, anyway?"

"Ten."

"What if you hook a musky or a big pike? You could hook one, you know; we've seen them hit those little minnow baits. But what are the chances that you'll land any with that gear? A pike or musky, even a little one, can bite through ten-pound mono like sewing thread. It'd be a shame to hook a big one and then lose it."

"I know," I said, "but I'm hurting to the point that I don't have much of a choice. My muscles are so tight that I'm afraid I won't be able to turn my head a half-inch one way or the other tomorrow, and I'll have to do my share of the driving. You guys keep after the muskies with your heavy gear if you want. I'm gonna see if I can catch a smallmouth or two."

But even though most of the spots we fished looked like classic smallmouth areas, I didn't have a single hit. In fact, for another few hours all we did was cast and retrieve, cast and retrieve, sneak a quick drink, eat a cookie or two, and then cast and retrieve. Things were so tough that I started calling up the details of what my last strike — from a rock bass back at the dock — felt like.

"It's about time," I finally said. "We've fished our way farther south down this side of the lake than I've ever been before, and I think we'd better start back. I don't want the other guys to have to start wondering where we are. Plus we need extra time tonight to get everything packed up for the drive tomorrow."

"One more spot, one more spot," Joel and Jason were almost chanting.

"Is there a good one fairly close?"

"Absolutely," Joel said without hesitating. "Down along the south side of Portage Bay there's this neat little cove with a big spread of subsurface rocks just off the middle of its mouth. Deep water on the outside. Shallower water and weeds on the inside."

"How do you know about it?"

"When Joel and I were guided last year," Jason said, "Mike showed it to us on our way back to camp. Since we were running late, we only tried a couple of casts. Didn't get anything then, but it looked great, and if we had had time for a few more casts last year, we would have nailed something for sure."

"You're the only two from our group who know anything about this spot?"

"Yeah," Jason went on. "Joel and I never said anything about it because we didn't have any hits there last year, and it's a good distance from camp. So far this year we haven't been back because we've been learning about so many spots farther north — around our own bay. But Mike said that once he and two clients were fishing that sunken rock island, and all three of them had a musky on at the same time. The spot looks as close to perfect as you're going to get. We should be able to find it. I remember that behind it on the shore of the cove was a stand of birches, and in front of the birches was a stretch of beach. Looked like sand from Holland or Grand Haven. Not a single rock or boulder on it."

"Can we get there in ten minutes or so? You're sure? Okay. We'll run down there, find the sunken island, give it a few casts, and then we're going to head back. And I don't want to hear any whining and complaining when I say it's time to leave. Okay, I'll run the motor — show me how to find this wonder spot."

Part of me expected to spend the next ten or fifteen minutes doing big circles in Portage Bay, arguing about whether what we saw in the distance was a peninsula or an island, losing track of what was south, feeling the first pulse of panic. But the boys found their way well across the big water and led me almost directly to the cove they hadn't seen in a year.

"We'll fish the edges," Joel said as he snapped on one of his new Llungen Tails. "If you're going to keep that little minnowbait on, you might as well toss it right up on top of the boulders and twitch it through them. There could be some smallmouth hiding up there."

I placed my first cast carefully, just to the left of the reddish brown of the rocks. Twitch, retrieve. Twitch, retrieve. Twitch, retrieve. Huh? What was that? Banged a rock. Twitch, retrieve. Nothing.

I put my second cast about six feet to the right of the first. Twitch . . . and my lure just stopped. *There must be some wood up there,* I thought. It felt as if I had pulled right into a stump or a log.

"Watch your casts," I told the boys. "I'm snagged up on top."

"Snap it," Joel said, impatient to cast again. "Peel off a little slack and then hold your rod as high as you can and snap the line. I don't think there's any wood up there. You must have run up on the back side of a boulder. Some slack and a snap, and it should come up and out."

I released the bail and peeled off some slack. I engaged the bail again, held the rod high, and gave my line a sharp yank. And then a musky, the biggest musky I have ever seen in the water and not mounted on some wall, erupted out of the water, spread its jaws, and shook its head violently — but failed to shake loose the front treble hook of my little Rebel minnow that was lodged in the corner of its mouth.

"You boys better find me some pills!" I yelled. "No way I can do anything with a fish like that with this gear."

Joel just groaned. "No fair, no fair. Why does it have to bite for the guy fishing with a peewee pole?"

"Wait! Just hold on a second," I said. "Crazy stuff happens sometimes. Look, she's just cruising along the front edge of the rocks. I can't really put any pressure on her, but maybe I can just ease her this way a little, nudge her to change direction and head toward us. There we go, baby. Look — she's turned. She's headed straight for us. She's swimming along calmly now, almost as if she doesn't know she's hooked. Joel, get the net ready. And Jase, see if you can get the rods on this side of the boat out of the way. I'm not gonna be able to stop this beast, and I'm not gonna be able to raise her head, but maybe I can put just enough pressure on her to get her to swim up close to us, and if she gets close, Joel, take a stab. Just take a deep stab and maybe we'll get her in the net. No one's gonna blame you if you miss. No other choice right now. Ready? Okay, she's coming this way. Here she comes. Look at those shoulders — I don't have hands big enough to grab hold of her! Closer, just a little bit closer. That's it. Just about ready."

And then there were flashes of action: Joel braced his hip against the motor. He extended the net as far out over the water as he could. The fish cruised straight toward me, then angled toward Joel. Joel made a violent swoop straight down with the net. The fish veered off, and Joel grunted. He thrust the rim of the net deeper and farther out. The fish hit the rim of the net and turned directly into the net. Then it swam ahead so hard that it got its snoot about three inches through the cords of the net but could go no farther because its shoulders were stuck. Jason let out a yelp and started using a seat as a drumhead. Joel pulled the net back to the boat and held the handle against the side, leaving the netted fish in the water. The fish thrashed so hard in the cords that it was beating a primitive rhythm on the side of the boat. All three of us leaned over and looked into the net. My eyes met Joel's.

"Oh, Dad! Oh, Dad! Just look at that thing!" Joel was almost choking.

For a few seconds I felt a slight swirl of dizziness. I concentrated on my breathing and then tried to focus again.

"This fish is in the net," I said, "but it's still as green as anything. With the pressure that I was able to put on it, it hardly had to fight. We're so lucky. This has to be one in a billion: we just eased the fish toward us and then stabbed at it and got it with the net. But now we're gonna have to be careful. This thing is so big and fresh it's scary. Where are my gloves? Let me get my gloves. Jase, you go into my bag and get the camera out. When you're ready, I'll unhook the musky and try to lift it up for some pictures. Not in that pocket — in the zippered one there on the side. See it? Okay, tell me when you're ready. The hook is in the cartilage, but I can get it with the pliers — it should twist out pretty easily. There."

"Dad," Jason's voice was quiet but insistent.

"What? I'm trying to get a grip on this thing. Just a second."

"Dad."

"What's the matter? You got the camera ready? Just get ready and I'll be able to lift this beast in a second. Don't get a finger in front of the lens."

"But, Dad."

"What? What's so hard about getting the camera ready?"

"Did you just stick the camera back in your bag after you used it for that attack this morning?"

"Yeah. So? Let's get going here. We can't keep this musky out of the water forever."

"It says we're out of exposures."

"What? You can't be serious. Are you looking at the right dial?"

"Absolutely. See — there's no number showing. You must have really gone crazy and used up all the film this morning."

"Oh, my goodness gracious alive!" I put the fish back into the net. "I catch the fish of about six lifetimes and I'm not going to get a single picture of it? Not one lousy picture! This can't be. I don't believe this is happening to me. Why does stuff like this have to happen to me? We don't have a single other camera in the boat? Huh? Joel, you got a camera?"

Joel gave a little shrug of resignation. Jason was putting my camera back in my tackle bag.

"Oh, oh, oh, oh! I'm so mad I could spit — could probably spit blood. Not one picture! And it's all my own dumb fault. I won't be able to show Jon and Duzzer and T-Gunz what this monster looks like. And Mom probably won't even believe I caught it. And this fish is so big that some magazine or newspaper would want to publish a picture of it. Probably a little story, too. And if I ever fall into an extra six hundred bucks or so, I won't even be able to get a reproduction of this fish because I won't be able to give the taxidermist enough details to work with. What am I supposed to do, draw him a picture? Write a little descriptive essay? Oh, I think I'd give an eyetooth for just one picture of this fish!"

"Dad, we'd better measure the fish and release it," Joel said, trying to hold the net and the fish away from the side of the boat.

"Yeah, yeah, yeah. Here, let me see. I'll hold it up, and you two guys measure it. Ready? There, I've got it. I've got a pretty good grip on it. What does it say? Hurry up — I can't hold this thing forever. It weighs about a ton. What does it say?"

"Fifty . . . fifty-three . . . ," Jason said, trying to hold the musky's tail still. "No, fifty-four inches, fifty-four inches on the nose. That's huge. Way to go, Dad. This is sure to be one of the biggest fish caught up here this summer. And you did it on light tackle. I wonder what the Ontario record for ten-pound test is. This has got to be some kind of record."

"Record, schmecord. Don't even remind me. Let's get this mama back in the water. How could I even begin to check if it's a record if I don't have one single picture of it? There. I can feel the strength in her muscles. There she goes, straight back toward those rocks. She's going to be fine. I wish I could say the same for me. Something inside is saying that it would have been better if I had never hooked that thing."

"No way, Dad," Joel said, shaking his head vigorously. "No way you should ever say that. You shouldn't even think that. You'll feel great about this catch in a day or two. You'll have good memories."

"I doubt it. I hate to have to tell you this, boys, but as you grow older, you can try and try and try some more, and you can even get lots of help from other people, but there are some things you just never get over."

About five months later, well into the darkest time of the year in Michigan, Joel was waiting for me inside the side door to our house when I came home from work in the early evening. As soon as I stepped inside, he thrust a magazine so close to my face that I could have taken a bite of it.

"Have you seen this?" he asked.

"No. What is it? *Musky Hunter?* Where'd you get it? We don't subscribe to that."

"Mom had to go to Schuler's after school, and I went along to check out the magazines. When I saw what was in this one, I about choked. You've got to see it. Toward the back. I'll find it. Where did it go? Just a second. Here."

"Slow down, slow down. Let me put these papers in my office and we'll sit down in the family room." After I'd put my things away and settled into my easy chair, I said, "Okay, what's got you so hot and bothered?"

Joel opened the *Musky Hunter* to a two-page spread of photos showing people holding muskies out in front of them at various angles.

"Tell me what you notice," Joel said, taking a step back.

"Well, let me see. What do I notice? A bunch of nice muskies . . ." Wanda walked into the room, followed by Jon and Jason.

"Have you seen it yet?" Wanda asked, walking over to kiss the top of my head.

"I see a bunch of pictures of muskies. And many of these fish, I have to say, aren't nearly as big as the one I had last summer. Yes, Wanda, no matter what you say, I did have the big one. And I caught it using — "

"Dad," Joel burst out, "look down in the left-hand corner."

I looked. There was a picture of three guys in a boat, a tall one standing with one hand under the gill plate of an enormous musky, a second standing next to the first and holding one end of a tape measure against the fish's jaw, the third kneeling and holding the tape measure along the fish's tail. Below the picture was a brief caption:

A pic of an Eagle Lake beauty, sent in anonymously.
Perhaps a father-and-sons effort.

As I read, the world turned upside down.

"How can this be? I don't get it. There's just no way. It's my fish, and there are the three of us for all the world to see. There you are, Joel. And Jason's reading the tape by the tail. You can't tell me this is possible. You guys said you never told a soul about that spot. And there wasn't anyone anywhere near us when I caught that fish. Something's just not right here. Are you guys playing some kind of computer trick on me, you know, Photoshop or something?"

"Dad, do you see that the picture is a little grainy?" Jason explained, as if the four of them had conferred ahead of time and agreed to take it slowly with me. "That means it was probably taken from quite a ways away, like with a telephoto lens. You can't believe how powerful those lenses are these days. How powerful are they anyway, Jon?"

"The first time I ever looked through one, I had a little trouble believing what I saw."

I was growing impatient. "Powerful, sure, but come on — think about this a little. Just listen to everything you're asking me to believe. Number one, you're telling me that there were some guys out on Eagle Lake with camera equipment powerful enough that they could get a picture of us from so far away that we didn't even have a clue they were around. Number two, you're implying that they must have had almost superhuman powers of perception, enough to notice that we had landed a fish just at that moment. Number three, you're suggesting that these guys would take the trouble to send that picture in to *Musky Hunter*. I've met some friendly anglers, sure, but anglers who would go out of their way to do that? Number four — "

"But we're not talking about some guys," Wanda said. "Just one." ☙

A Friend Indeed

It all started a few weeks after I had bought my boat. I had coaxed Wanda into taking a ride up to some lakes in northern Kent County — Murray, Big Pine Island, and Wabasis. My only motivation was a case of persistent uneasiness. I had had no experience backing up a boat on a trailer, so before I actually drove into a launch site and started looking like a fool, I wanted to check out the launch sites on some of the lakes fairly close to home to learn which ones were large enough to let me swing my boat trailer around fairly smoothly and get its wheels onto the concrete ramp leading into the water. Jon and Jason were at their friends' houses that night, so Wanda and I made a special point of asking Joel if he wanted to ride along with us. But a ride with his parents, even though we held out promises of an ice-cream cone, maybe even one of those huge ice-cream cones from the general store in Smyrna, wasn't on his list that night. He begged to stay home and practice some jumps on his dirt bike down in the woods by Plaster Creek with his friend Nick. Nick's mom, so Joel told us, had said something about Joel's coming inside with Nick if we didn't get home until after dark.

Something went more wrong that night than I used to be able to imagine was possible within the frame of a single summer evening. Our drive to the three launch sites took about forty-five minutes longer than I had expected. We learned later that, after taking only a few jumps, Nick got tired of fighting off mosquitoes and left Joel by himself in the woods. A few minutes later, Joel himself left the woods and pedaled home. There he found all the doors and windows to our house closed and locked. Once he knew he couldn't get inside, he remembered nothing about the offer from Nick's mom but decided his only option was to sit on the front porch and try a game to fight off the looming demons: close his eyes and rest his head on his knees while counting to one hundred and then look up and peer down the street to see if any headlights were swinging around the corner. Then close his eyes and count to a hundred again. And again. But as he said later that night, "You didn't come and you didn't come — I lost track of all the hundreds." Finally, he also told us, some voice in his head suggested that, whether we had veered off the road and drowned in some ditch or had wandered across the center line and been crushed by a semi, we had somehow managed to get ourselves killed and to leave him abandoned. Thus when Wanda and I pulled into the driveway at last, we could make out a huddled form on our front porch, a form that jumped up, ran over to me as I got out of the car, wrapped itself around my left leg, and would not let me go.

Before that night, I always thought that something as damaging to a person as separation anxiety could be brought on only by momentous and dramatic occasions, by events that would lead other people to look away from the victim and whisper behind shielding hands, "Thank God that didn't happen to us!" But that wasn't true for the actions that wounded Joel. Everything about that night seemed both trivial and circumstantial. Why should it have mattered that I got out of the car at all of the launch sites to pace off the width of the launching areas? Why should it have made any difference that I hit several red lights as I drove south on the East Beltline on our way home? Why should it have been of any importance that Nick, thinking only about mosquitoes leaving welts on his arms, forgot to give Joel even a brief reminder that he could come over to his house once he was tired of riding in the woods?

I have worked at it, but I can find no good answer to these questions. I only know that our delay damaged Joel where the damage would fester. This son, the one who had been so competitive, so confident about his abilities, so willing to make his own way and take on whatever challenges had ever come up in his young life, had been transformed in one night into a boy who needed to have Wanda or me near him almost every one of his waking moments.

As our family managed to put some months between us and the night of separation, Wanda and I were relieved to notice that Joel was starting to experience some small measures of healing. He could roam around the neighborhood for twenty minutes or so and join in a basketball game at the end of the street. He even challenged himself to ride up to his school, four blocks away. There, he said, he would spend some time twisting on swings and walking out on teeter-totters, trying to find the balance point.

But in two ways he continued to show that he was not the same Joel who had begged us to let him stay home and ride bikes with Nick. For one thing, almost every time he came back into the house after being outside, his talk was limited to one sentence form, the question:

"Is Mom here? Where's Mom?"

"I think she went shopping for a little while."

"You think? Don't you know? When did you see her last?"

"I'm pretty sure she said she had to stop at a store or two."

"What store? Do you know what she needed?"

"I'm not sure. She said she was going to check out a few different things."

"So when's she gonna get back? How long's she been gone already? Did she say when she'd be back?"

"Just ease up a little, okay? Mom's knees keep her from being the queen of all shoppers, but she does like to get out a little bit. She's probably just at some memory-book store. She'll be back before too long."

"How can you be so sure? Did she tell you all that before she left? Did she call you or something?"

For another thing, he became uncompromisingly restrictive about the places he would let me take him fishing. In the years leading up to that night, I had taken my family to some famous bodies of water located as far away as the Upper Peninsula. And I kept wanting to extend the range of our fishing excursions farther and farther to the north. After that night, Joel never wanted to travel to lakes that were more than thirty minutes from home. I liked lakes with channels snaking between islands and leading to little fingers of water cut back into the shoreline on unpredictable angles. After that night, Joel never wanted to fish any lake where the launch site wasn't visible from every spot on the lake. I liked lakes with as much undeveloped shoreline as possible, with herons waiting and watching among the reeds, abandoned beaver lodges gradually collapsing into themselves, and osprey nests overlooking bays. After that night, Joel never wanted to fish a lake without cottages, preferably newer cottages complete with boathouses and gazebos, along the entire shoreline. I liked lakes that were so still that I could watch the surface for reflections of cumulus shape-shifters. After that night, Joel never was comfortable on lakes that weren't churning with activity, lakes with ski jumps and bright buoys marking slalom courses, lakes with speedboats circling to pick up five-year-olds who had fallen off boards and tubes, lakes that were stirred into a froth by the intersecting wakes of jet skis.

When Joel and I fished together, anything out of the ordinary could be trouble. Even the seemingly small things — a growl of thunder in the distance — would make him quiet, tense, jittery. And the bigger things — the motor coughing and threatening not to start once we were out of sight of a launch area — could throw him into a full-blown panic: he would usually wail and try to wedge himself into the small storage space under the casting deck in the bow of the boat.

Yet, no matter how bad his panic ever seemed, I resisted the thought of not taking him on fishing trips. I knew I wouldn't be able to pull out of the driveway with Jon and Jason and have to look back over my shoulder and see the outline of Joel's face in the picture window. Even to imagine him resigning himself to staying behind triggered my most intense protective instincts.

But I also sensed that I needed to show some patience, to bide my time, to wait for more healing. So for a year or two after the night of separation, I didn't even hint to him about trips to the U.P. or Canada. Nor did I talk much about possible visits to my brother and his family on Douglas Lake, up near Pellston. I focused on getting him to extend the range of lakes he would consider fishing within reasonable driving distance from home.

As Joel grew older, however, I put some little schemes into play. I bought copies of fishing magazines that published stories about almost unimaginably large pike and muskies in big lakes, especially lakes in Wisconsin, Minnesota, the Upper Peninsula, and Ontario. I would then leave them lying around the house where he could find them. I ordered copies of videos about pike and musky fishing and started to watch them when I knew Joel was home. I sent away for hydrographic maps of such famous Ontario lakes as Eagle, Lac Seul, and Lake of the Woods, and I'd leave them spread out on the floor of the basement. When I took the boys to bait stores, I spent most of my time in the aisle with the big baits: the Grandmas, the Suicks, the Believers.

"I sure hope you're not trying to be subtle," Joel said, coming up alongside me in Dick's Sporting Goods as I sorted through some jerkbaits.

"Subtle?"

"Why don't you just come right out and tell me you want to take us way up north someplace? Get it out in the open. Just so you know it's not gonna do any good. I can't go fishing so far away. You know that would freak me out. Why don't you just go with Jon and Jason?"

"Joel, there's no way I would ever go on a big fishing trip and leave you behind."

"Yeah, right."

"It absolutely is right. You've got to accept that. And I think that deep down you really would like to hook into a fish about as big as you are. So I believe we should brainstorm about some ways for you to get over what happened. I'm not sure what would work best. You got any ideas? I did wonder whether it would help for you to take one of your buddies along. I'd be happy to pay for an extra person. The two of you could share a boat, and you could carry on all day long about the stuff you usually jabber about. Maybe it would seem as if the two of you were just monkeying around like you do on ponds around town here. I think that might help . . . maybe it would help a lot. What about it?"

"Maybe. I hadn't thought of that. I'll see."

Every two or three weeks after that, I would wait for a time when the two of us were alone together and then ask him how his thinking about my proposal was coming along. But it was not until a year later that he finally decided to take one of the bigger risks of his life: he agreed to consider a trip to Ontario.

"You must have thought about what I said before. Do you want to take a friend? Have you talked to anybody?"

"Yeah, I talked to Trout, and he seems pretty interested. Since his family moved into their new house on that lake in Grandville, he's been fishing quite a bit."

"Trout?"

"Yeah, you know — Justin. Everyone calls him Trout."

"How come? I don't remember many freckles."

"Nothing to do with freckles. It goes all the way back to a recess period during sixth grade. We were out on Millbrook's court playing hoops, and he pulls this awesome little move in the post. In sixth grade he was taller than anyone else and always played down low. At one point he gives a little drop step and then pivots around his guy and makes a reverse lay-up, and we're all just going nuts. 'What's everybody yappin' about?' he yells out. 'Don't you know I'm so fast because I have the reflexes of a fish?' And then Postie chimes in, 'No fair! We're playing against a trout!' The name just stuck. Anyways, he's been doin' some fishing off the dock at his new house, and he thinks he's Joe expert fisherman."

"Do you think he'd make a good fishing partner for you up north?"

"Maybe. As you can probably tell from the basketball story, he's really cocky. So he won't listen to anyone about how to fish. I've been fishing for years more than he has, but he won't take any advice from me. He's always got to do everything his own crazy way. For sure he doesn't do anything the way you and Duzzer would."

"Give me an example."

"Well, for one thing, you won't believe what he uses for bait."

"What? Grasshoppers . . . crickets?"

"Nope. He takes sections of hot dogs and puts them on the hook. He says they're so deadly for bass they're illegal in most tournaments."

"You can't be serious. Kernels of corn, sure, and balls of dough and stuff like that for carp. But not hot dogs! Don't tell me he says they plump under water."

"After a while they just get real soggy and fall off the hook. So if you fish for a while, you've got to keep a pack of fresh hot dogs in the bait box or cooler."

"That's one of the grossest things I've ever heard. And you say that a lot of what he does while fishing is wacky?"

"Yup. You should see him stand on the front edge of his family's pontoon boat and pretend with his six-foot spinning rod that he's some kind of hotshot fly fisherman."

"Sounds like he's setting himself up for trouble. But our issue right now is how you and Trout would manage in a boat together up north. You thought about that? Will it be okay?"

"Can't say for sure. But whenever I fish with him at his lake, he's a riot to watch. Just about everything he does is funny."

"Maybe he'll be a distraction — you know — maybe he'll keep you from letting the bad stuff get into your head."

"That's what I'm hoping . . ."

"Still, hijinks on a lake in Grandville are one thing. Hijinks on a lake hours away might be another."

"I know, Dad, but I'm hoping it won't matter. You should see the stuff he does."

"Okay, but we've got to be absolutely clear about this. Are you saying I should go ahead and start looking for a fishing camp in Canada? I don't want to send off a deposit and then have to back out and lose it."

"I brought this up mainly so you could get started. You think I don't want to get over this? But you'd better look for a camp we can drive to. I don't think I could handle a fly-in."

"That's fine by me. I'm sure there are lots of great camps up around Lake Superior. You get to all of them by road — good paved roads."

A few months later found my three sons and me loading our gear into a rented van extremely early one Saturday morning, swinging over to Grandville to pick up Trout, and then setting out for Little Vermillion Lake, near Sioux Lookout, Ontario.

The trip got me thinking that having Trout along was going

to be great. His mom had filled an empty ice-cream bucket with home-baked M&M cookies, and once Trout let the rest of us try them, I had to appoint myself official keeper of the cookies to make sure that no one got more than his fair share.

And once we got north of Cedar Springs and past the heaviest traffic, Trout came up with a great travel game.

"Everybody think of your top three movies of all time and rank them one through three, with one tops. Then each of us takes a turn reporting and gives reasons for his choices."

So after a few minutes of such intense concentration that we could hear one another breathing, one of the boys would start with his list and then conclude it by saying something like, "My number-one movie of all time is — ta-da, ta-da — *Dumb and Dumber*."

"Oh, yeah!" one of the others would respond. "That's great. How did I forget that! I never gave it a thought. That scene with the bikini team was the funniest thing I've ever seen. It was awesome."

"Have Mom and I wasted years of private schooling on you kids?" I cut in. "I'd hate to add up how much we've paid in tuition over the years. Guess we would have been better off putting that money into a cottage. How could you have gotten that education and then actually come up with *Dumb and Dumber* for your list?"

Mile after mile went by like that, from memories of our top three athletic achievements, through anecdotes about our three meanest teachers, to memories of our top three most embarrassing moments — the claims, the questions, the howls, the groans, the shrieks of laughter, the near choking, the shoulder-punching, the massaging of tightened neck muscles, the wiping of runny noses. And although we didn't pay proper attention to the vistas outside our windows, the afternoon and early evening passed like a waking dream, and we arrived at the camp, which featured a large rustic lodge and several smaller cabins, early enough to unload our gear, eat a few cookies and chips, and head out for an hour or so of fishing.

We motored around the back side of the island nearest the lodge, Joel and Trout in one boat, Jason and Jon with me in another. Soon after we settled into bobbing fifteen or twenty yards off the crowns of blown-down cedar trees lying in the water along the shore, Trout gave me additional reasons to believe that inviting him along had been a great idea. He had rigged himself up with a silver-and-black floating Rapala, and on the second twitch after landing this bait between two downed trees, he was fighting his first Canadian smallmouth bass. He lost that fish in the branches, but it turned out that he and Joel soon discovered an extensive spread of smallmouth beds, many of them under or just to the side of downed tree trunks, and all they had to do was flip floating baits near these beds to trigger strikes that were startling in their aggressiveness.

Because the first instinct of those hooked bass was to swim back and try to wrap the line around nearby branches, Joel and Trout didn't land all the fish they hooked. But they did walk up from the dock to the cabin later that night almost feverish with excitement about their catch: several small bass and six that exceeded twenty inches, the minimum standard for master-angler smallmouth in that district of Ontario.

This is going to be great, I thought as I flossed before bed. *Sometimes you almost have to give yourself a little pinch to make sure you're not dreaming.* The next morning, however, was like a chop between the shoulder blades. Since we didn't want to beat up on spawning fish, we decided not to go back to the bedding territory that Joel and Trout had discovered the night before. Instead, we thought we'd try a bay that was about a mile out from the lodge, a bay that looked on the map like an anvil. Once in the mouth of the bay, we decided that Joel and Trout would move down the shoreline first, while Jon, Jason, and I would wait a few minutes and then follow, casting different baits. This tactic, we had heard back in camp, was called "raking the water."

Even before they were thirty yards down the shoreline, I could see that Trout was going to be trouble. Either he had not learned how to start his retrieve quickly enough after casting, or he just wasn't bothering to do so. The night before, the slow start to his retrieves hadn't caused any trouble because he had been casting a floating minnow. This morning, though, Trout had settled on using a bucktail spinner. A skilled angler using a bucktail along a shoreline with rocks and boulders strewn about would cast the spinner and then engage the reel and start retrieving the lure as soon as it hit the water. But Trout was casting his spinner, letting it sink into the rocks, reaching over to take a swig of Mountain Dew, turning toward Joel to crack a joke, engaging the reel, and then preparing to start the retrieve. Sometimes he succeeded. But often he was snagged: his bucktail would sink and get wedged between heavy rocks. So we could see Joel positioning the boat near where Trout's line had disappeared into the water; and then we'd watch Trout yanking on his line while Joel used an oar to reach into the water and try to free the spinner.

I sat thirty or forty yards away from Joel and Trout, feeling a little guilty about what I was bothering God about, but nevertheless pleading with him for one thing and one thing only: *Please keep Trout's spinner out of all the cracks and crevices.* But it seemed that when Trout wasn't snagged on the bottom, he was casting too far or on the wrong angle, whipping his lure into the weathered arms of dead trees in the water along the shore. For a joke, Jason took a picture of Joel and Trout's boat as it was nosed right in among the fallen timber, Joel leaning over trying to steady the boat by grasping branches that weren't under the surface, Trout kneeling in the bow and stretching forward trying to get his line out of the branches.

After they had spent almost ten minutes struggling to get Trout's spinner out of a downed tree, I proposed motoring on to a rocky point I saw in the distance and taking an early shore lunch. Joel was shaking his head.

"Go ahead and lead the way over there," I yelled, "and don't either of you take any more casts on the way. We need a break from all this fussing in the branches and the rocks."

When I hopped out of the boat and wrapped a mooring line around a jagged boulder, I noticed that Joel was already out on the tip of the point, fancasting the water in front of him. He was working himself into a frenzy. I hopped boulders until I was at his side.

"Whoa, whoa, whoa. Don't you think you'd better slow down? Cast like that and you'll wear yourself out in half a day. What's up, anyway?"

"Dad, here we drive for hours up to Canada — I've got to get a little fishing in. Did you see us this morning? That was a joke! I try to take a cast or two, and then I hear Trout: 'Joel, I'm snagged again, out at the end of that dead tree with all the moss on it. Can you pooch me over there? Guess I don't know my own strength!' I don't think I got six casts in the whole time. No way I'm going to be able to hack this."

"Hold on a minute. We don't have to fish along shorelines. We can move out in the bays or in the mouths of bays and look for deeper weed beds."

"Dad, I'm already uneasy as all get out. I try to ignore it, I try to shrug it off, but every now and then I get lightheaded. I keep feeling like something awful is going to happen, but I can't say what it is. Maybe it's that you and Mom are going to die. And all of a sudden I get super self-conscious. There I was watching myself turning the crank on my reel, trying not to, but still counting the exact number of times I would twitch the rod tip on each retrieve. Don't tell me you know how I feel because you don't. You just don't. Nobody does. I can't just do something, I can't just live, but I have to sort of float above myself and watch myself doing every little thing. It's awful. And just before we broke for lunch, I started worrying about finding our way back to the lodge. I can't remember half the channels we went through. And we're so far from home. I don't know what I'm going to do with myself."

I fought back. "Joel, we'll find our way back. I've got a pretty good picture of the route in my head. Right now let's get something in our stomachs. And then this afternoon we'll take that channel the dock boy was talking about and follow it all the way to Maskinonge Lake. I hear that Maskinonge was a provincial musky sanctuary — no fishing allowed — until just a few years ago. So I'm guessing the muskies in there will like what we throw at them."

"I'll try, but this is feeling more and more like one of those nightmares that wake me up in a sweat only a half hour or so after I've finally fallen asleep. I can't believe I ever said I'd come up here."

The channel to Maskinonge made its serpentine way through marsh grass and small clusters of stunted firs. Shortly after the channel widened to the point that we were sure we were actually on a small bay of Maskinonge, we killed the motors, let ourselves drift, and studied the lake maps we had picked up in the lodge.

"Look at this point, probably straight across from where we are now," Jason said, showing me on the map. "It's classic. It drops off along both sides to what looks like thirty feet of water in a matter of yards. I'll bet it's a long slab of rock laid down in the water. We've got to find it. You know the fish are going to be roaming back and forth along the sides of a piece of rock like that."

"Follow us!" I yelled to Joel and Trout. "Jason's spotted what looks like a great underwater point. I think it should be just to the right of that rock face across there."

The point turned out to be easy to find. But when we rowed up close enough to see exactly what it looked like, we realized that Jason had been right about the steepness of the edges and the depth of water that it extended into, but wrong about what it was made up of. It was not a large slab of rock but a mass of medicine-ball-sized boulders stacked up steeply. We could see them massed in the water for at least fifteen or twenty feet before they disappeared into the dark.

"This looks even better than I had imagined," I whispered to Jon and Jason. "More hiding places than along a slab. Let's row back out and decide how we're going to fish this."

Once we were far enough out from the boulders so that we

wouldn't disturb any fish with noises or shadows from the boats, we held the boats together and came up with a plan.

"See how the wind is moving across the point from right to left?" I said, pointing it out. "Why don't we both motor off to the right, and then take turns drifting across the point? We'll have to make sure to stay out deep enough so that the fish don't sense us. Then we can cast in on both sides of the ramp. Any place with as many nooks and crannies as this ramp has — plus there's deep water on both sides — should hold a ton of fish. Our job is to drift along and pick them off one by one. Probably we should put on deep-running baits the first couple of drifts across and work the outside. Then we can move in a little, switch to shallower stuff, and cast up along the top and almost to shore. Sound okay?"

Everyone nodded. We moved both boats upwind from the point and flipped a coin to see who got to make the first drift. Joel and Trout won, and Jon, Jason, and I watched expectantly as they swung their boat parallel to the shoreline, drifted away from us, stood up, and started to cast.

"Oo-nay! Ah-nay! Ach-tay! Pewanamo!" Jon and Jason tried to help them out by quietly chanting the refrain from a fish-catching song we had heard on a DVD about salmon fishing in Alaska. "Oo-nay! Ah-nay! Pow!"

Jon's arm shot out: "There!" Joel's rod snapped into a tight arc, and a heavy fish boiled fifteen yards off their boat. We strained to make it out.

"It's gotta be a big pike," Jason said, looking like he was ready to dive in and swim over for a better look. "See Joel? He's reeling like crazy. That fish must be running for the boat, and big pike do that all the time."

"You're the family expert on big pike?" Jon shot back, heavy with sarcasm. "Pike aren't the only fish that charge — "

Just then Joel's fish exploded out of the water and twisted its body so severely in the air that if it had wanted to, it could have bitten its own tail.

"Ah, now, now I see," Jason said. His body was rigid. "It's a musky, a tiger musky! Look at those stripes! That's the first tiger any of us has ever hooked."

Joel and Trout's boat was floating in fairly deep water off the point, so there was a limit to the tricks the musky could pull on Joel, and after about ten minutes we could see the musky thrashing in the net off the side of their boat.

"Our turn now," Jon said, turning toward me. "Let's get one."

We pulled the anchor and started our drift. Jason was casting a weighted Suick, Jon had a magnum silver Bomber, and I had my patched-up black-and-orange Bull Dawg.

"Just remember," I reminded them, "we're fishing the deeper water first. Don't toss anything in shallow or up on top yet. We'll save that for later drifts. First let's call up whatever's down in the dark."

We stood and began to cast, the muscles in our forearms almost twitching in anticipation of a strike.

Then a little "ungh!" came from my left side. It was Jon, who lost his balance and went down on one knee after setting the hook.

"Did you nail him?" I yelled as he scrambled to get back to his feet.

"I'm pretty sure I did. It was like setting into a horse! Look out! Here he comes. He's coming up. He's coming up fast."

And then his fish, another tiger muskie, probably a few inches longer and certainly several pounds heavier than Joel's, did a somersault in the air, shook its head violently, and spat Jon's Bomber out of its mouth with so much force that it shot back halfway to us.

The three of us sat down as one, and Jon cupped his hands around his face.

"Did you see that? Did you see that? That fish went wacko," Jason said, sliding his camera back into its waterproof pouch.

"It was like somebody collected half the nastiness in all of Ontario and stuffed it into that one fish," I said. "It all happened so fast, it's like my brain is still trying to sort everything out. Goodness, Jon — have you ever seen anything like that before? This kind of action is going to give you high blood pressure."

"All I know . . . all I know is . . ." Jon seemed trapped between grief and anger. "It's a mighty good thing that happened on our first pass. I see we've drifted a ways past the point. Let's get going. Go back up and make another drift. Joel and Trout are just starting their second pass. Something bad is going to happen if one of them messes with that fish before I get another crack at it."

I fired up the motor and veered off well outside of Joel and Trout. Then we sat and watched them for the second time.

"What's he doing? Is he nuts?" Jason's voice was near a growl. He was staring across the water at Trout, who had stood up in their boat to cast. Nothing unusual about that. But he was not standing on the floor of the boat; instead, he had one foot on one gunnel and the other foot across the boat on the other gunnel, quite close to the bow. And he seemed to be imitating a fly fisherman, leaving about six inches of line between his rod tip and his lure as he swept his rod back and forth from about ten o'clock to two. Finally, he gave a really exaggerated sweeping motion and apparently tried to release the bail of his reel and cast his lure out along the rock pile. But his bail didn't release, and because of that, Trout lost his balance up on the gunnels, swayed back and forth and swung his rod wildly to try to steady himself. But he ultimately could not avert what he had set in motion, and he fell out of the boat.

"Can you believe it? Just look at that!" Jon said. He was as irritated as I've ever seen him. Trout was in no real trouble. The air temperature was about eighty degrees, the water was easily seventy, and he was in the shallow water above the boulder pile. So it's hard to explain the absolute frenzy of splashing and wallowing that Trout went through before he hauled himself back into the boat with Joel.

Once Joel had backed their boat off the point, we rowed over to them.

"Probably we should get Trout some dry clothes," Joel said. It was obvious that he was trying to steady his breathing. "But I don't think . . . I don't think I can find the way back to camp by myself."

"That's all right," I said. "Whatever fish were here are bound to be long gone by now anyway. We'll all go back to camp together. After we get back, maybe I'll fire up the grill for an early supper and then after that we can talk about what we should do tonight."

On the way back I couldn't get my mind off what might have been. I was sure that if Joel had caught a few more tiger muskies like that one, he'd be so pumped that he'd be able to travel anywhere to fish. But I had never seen anything like what

I had witnessed that afternoon. More than once I had seen anglers lose their balance in rivers and stumble and take water over the tops of their waders. But rocking on the gunnels and pretending to be fly-fishing with spinning equipment and a big-lipped diving bait? English doesn't have a word for something worse than *embarrassing*.

Back at the dock, I stayed in our boat for a minute or two as the boys scrambled up the hill to our cabin, Trout making little squishy noises as he went. I had to sort out some lures, I told them. But my lures didn't need sorting. *So close. We were so close*, I said to myself. *Why can't things just work out? Why can't they work out just once? But maybe, if I get going and grill up some hot dogs and brats, I can get Joel back out there today and we can tie into another tiger or two.*

While I was hunched over on the deck of our cabin trying to start the grill, Joel sneaked up on me and let his desperation out: "There's no way I'm going to make it through this whole week up here. It won't make a bit of difference if we're hooking fish every minute. I'm not going to be able to take it."

"Was it really that bad? That was a beautiful tiger you caught."

"Sure, but have you forgotten the rest of it? For one thing, I go almost all morning with hardly a cast, just helping Trout get unsnagged. First he's in the rocks. Then he's in tree branches. One time he left a bunch of slack line in the water and I almost started taking it up with the propeller. And then after we move and I have that beautiful tiger, he goes and falls out of the boat. He falls out of the stinking boat! Can you believe that? I tried, Dad, you know I tried, but I can't do this. I can't take any more of this. This is bad stuff, Dad. If I have to stay here, I'm going to come apart."

So many emotions hit me then that I wasn't sure I could sort them out and name them. But impatience was certainly there, impatience in the face of a young boy who could dribble a soccer ball forty or fifty yards, evading defenders who were trying to steal the ball, but who couldn't go to Ontario for a family fishing vacation. And maybe anger. I think there might have been some anger that was rooted in what I sensed even then was an outdated and hurtful view of emotional damage, a view that I knew I needed to change, a view that held that, if people suffered emotionally, they were suffering mainly from a lack of willpower. To too great an extent, I was still under the spell of a cliché from my youth: "Feeling bad? It's a matter of choice." And maybe I even felt a spike of guilt: Was there something, I worried, deep within my genes or associated with my fathering that had contributed to Joel's paralyzing fear? I couldn't come up with any good answers, but I had to respond to Joel.

"How about letting me try to deal with some of the fear for you? Let's get supper ready. And then instead of rushing back out on the water, maybe we should all try to relax and get some extra sleep tonight. I brought a bunch of fishing magazines for you to look at to take your mind off yourself before you fall asleep. And then tomorrow we'll just stay on the go all day long. Sometimes the best thing to do in situations like this is to stay super busy. How about giving that a try?"

"I don't know, I don't know."

"We can at least try it, can't we? What do you think? Let me worry about setting up an agenda that will keep us hopping."

"Well, maybe just for tomorrow. I didn't sleep much last night, so maybe I'll be pooped when I get in bed tonight. If I can just make it to tomorrow, maybe we can see if your plan will work at all."

Somehow Joel managed to fall asleep that night. And by setting an almost frenetic pace, I managed to get him through the next day. We would motor up to a rocky point or a bed of weeds and cast, cast, cast. If someone hooked something — usually a pike — we would stay on that spot for another fifteen or twenty casts. But if we got no hint of action for seven or eight minutes, I would unfold the map, yell out to the other boat that we were moving on, and lead them off to a new spot. Once we had been to four or five spots and had had no action whatsoever, we headed back to the dock. There we secured the boats and got in the van and drove to Sioux Lookout. Once in town, we stopped at all the bait stores to examine lures, visited a grocery store and bought some magazines and candy bars, checked out the menus at all the restaurants along Main Street, visited the office of some bush pilots and learned how much it would cost to rent various outpost cabins for a week (pretending that flying to an outpost cabin was something that Joel could ever do), and learned from a regional conservation officer about dozens of local lakes that we could bounce along two-tracks to and wade in to fish. Each subsequent day, in addition to Little Vermillion Lake, I took the boys to two or three of these small lakes, where we waded and caught some pike and an occasional smallmouth.

Through the week, then, we roared from spot to spot on Little Vermillion Lake. We tried out almost all the lures in our tackle boxes. We took rides in the van. We compared prices for French and Greek dinners with names we were unable to pronounce or translate. We shopped. We stopped at gas stations for snacks. We talked to dozens of different people. We took hikes. We looked for agates in deserted quarry holes. We waded in and fished several lakes.

Joel got through the week without coming apart, at least as

far as any of the others could tell. But as for me, I suspected that it would take me at least a month to rest up from this weeklong vacation. But worse, I feared that one of my dreams for the future was never going to come true. I worried that in coming years it would probably take a clear miracle for my three sons and me to explore lakes other than those near Grand Rapids.

For the rest of that summer, as the boys and I fished lakes close to home, I tried hard not to think about lakes where huge muskies lurked along rocky points. And during the following fall, especially around the time of Joel's birthday in September, I reminded myself that it wasn't fair to keep putting pressure on him, asking him to travel to places that I would love to explore but that would almost certainly trigger his anxiety.

But by the following February, the time of year when my craving to get a line in the water becomes gnawingly intense, it occurred to me that having Joel take a friend along on a trip to Ontario was not necessarily a bad idea. We just had to make sure it was the right friend, someone who could cast with a modest amount of skill and wouldn't try crazy stunts in a fishing boat. What had been a riot for Joel to watch in Grandville had turned out to be a disaster on a big lake in Ontario.

I had noticed that when Joel was watching TV by himself downstairs, he would slip in an *In-Fisherman* musky videotape and turn the volume way down. But I could hear enough through the vents to know what he was watching. And why he was watching. Despite his trauma up at Little Vermillion Lake the prior summer, some musky fever was on him.

Tommy! Tommy might be the one! I thought, congratulating myself on the idea. *He might never have fished in his life, but it's clear that if he wants to learn something, he works hard at it and learns it. And he's so agile that I think those boys would have to get their boat sideways in storm waves to knock him overboard. Joel should invite Tommy.*

Tommy — commonly known as T-Gunz — was a little older than Joel, but they had become close friends playing on the same soccer team for several seasons. As they matured, each came close to defining a different position on the team.

T-Gunz was a striker. He was so quick with the ball that from the stands he often appeared not to be running and dribbling but flitting — erratically flitting — from spot to spot, the ball somehow attached to his feet. He was entirely unpredictable in his pace: at times he would jog, seemingly in aimless little circles, and during those times defenders probably thought that all the reports about his skill were manufactured by T-Gunz himself. But then, without any perceptible notice, he would dart to an open area, suddenly putting five or six yards between himself and the defender, and collect a pass from a teammate without any kind of physical challenge. And when he had the ball in front of the opposition's goal, he was as patient, as calm, and ultimately as deadly as any predator, human or animal.

Joel was a central midfielder. He was dominant in the air, winning headballs while opponents tried one illegal tactic after another to try to stop him: draping an arm across his shoulders, grasping his jersey or shorts as he went up, and elbowing him in the small of the back while he was in the air. He had an uncanny sense — an extra sense, really — of the spots where the defense could be attacked. And he could send passes to teammates with such startling accuracy that I would sometimes catch my breath as the ball somehow threaded through opponents' legs and found the leading foot of a teammate.

The most striking thing about watching T-Gunz and Joel play soccer together was that each apparently had a constant and confident sense of where the other was at any given moment and where he would be in a few seconds. Joel could have his back to T-Gunz as he would receive a pass from one of his teammates, and then could fight off the mugging of an opponent or two, whirl, yell "Gunz!" — and without hesitation send a ball directly into the path that T-Gunz had started on several seconds earlier. And T-Gunz could fake to the inside, carry the ball toward the sideline, outrace opponents to a corner flag, and then send a cross pass in front of the net so that Joel, sprinting down the center of the field, was set up perfectly for a scoring header.

Why didn't I come up with this idea before? I asked myself. *Joel and T-Gunz are so good together, they'd probably be a perfect team up north.*

And then my mind offered me a second gift. *It'll never work for me to start bugging Joel about Canada again. He'll know what I'm up to. I should get T-Gunz to do that for me.*

So after a Saturday soccer game in the early spring, I sought T-Gunz out and did some work while none of my sons was around.

"Hey, T., you know how much the boys and I like to fish, right? You ever done any fishing yourself?"

"Nope. I used to bug my dad about it. But all he thinks about is fast-pitch softball. Teach me how to bunt, sure, but no way he'll ever take me fishing."

"Well, if someone were to take you along fishing sometime, do you think you'd enjoy it? Do you think you'd be good at it?"

"I'd work hard to be good at it."

"Really?"

"Yup. And whatever I couldn't figure out on my own, I'm sure Joel would help me with. He's a pretty good teacher."

"So what do you think about coming along with the boys, Duzzer, and me this summer on a weeklong trip to Canada? I'd be happy to pay for another person."

"Lots of fish there?"

"Lots of fish . . . big fish. Make a cast and brace yourself so that you don't have your shoulders yanked out of their sockets. Thing is, though, before we go I would need a little help from you."

"What?"

"Well, Joel had a bad experience in Canada last summer. I don't know if he's ever talked to you about it. He asked Trout along — you know Trout, right? — and Trout spent his time up there either snagging his line or falling out of the boat. It was all so crazy that Joel started freaking out. So if a summer trip sounds good to you, you should work on Joel so that he's willing to give Canada another try."

"I'm supposed to bring Joel back for you?"

"I need somebody to do it."

"Okay, I'll give it a shot. But two things: You can't say anything about this to Joel. Don't tell him we talked. And if I get him to go, don't ever ask either of us how I did it."

"Why not? What're you thinking of?"

"Not gonna say."

"But — "

"As our coach always says, no 'buts' allowed. Just wait and see what happens."

To this day I have no idea what Tommy ever said or did to

Joel. All I know is, about a month after Tommy and I talked, Joel found me in my study and told me that he wanted to give Canada one more try. Also, he said, he wanted to take a friend along, a different friend this time, T-Gunz.

I honored my promise and never said a word to Joel about the little scheme that T-Gunz and I had put into play. And though my curiosity was a steady itch, I never tried to find out what tactics T-Gunz used. Knowing that we could never return to Little Vermillion, the site of so much trauma for Joel, I busied myself with finding a new fishing camp. I did some research and made some calls and arranged to rent a cabin at a camp on Eagle Lake, west of Little Vermillion, almost to Manitoba.

The first part of our day-and-a-half drive to Eagle was drizzly, the sky a rippled slab of dark slate, and after a few taunts and some outrageous predictions about fishing success, my boys settled into various contorted positions in the back of our rented van and started to make the wheezes and whistles of immature snorers. But T-Gunz had apparently packed several electronic games in his overnight bag, and as we headed north to the straits, my friend Duzzer, behind the steering wheel, and I, in the copilot's seat, could hear all kinds of beeps, chirps, whistles, and strings of burps coming from the seat just behind us.

Somewhere near where we made the cut over to I-75, between Mancelona and Lake Otsego, T-Gunz started with a series of questions:

"How fast are we going right now?"

I glanced to my left. "About sixty-two, sixty-three — seven

or eight miles over the speed limit," Duzzer said. "Probably just below what would get us a ticket." He grinned.

"Okay, good. Sounds about right. And how far do you think we are from Gaylord?"

"Why? We're not planning to stop in Gaylord," I said. "You need a pit stop already? I made a big point of telling everyone to use the john before we hit the road."

"No, no, I'm just curious. How far would you say it is to Gaylord?"

"Don't know for sure," said Duzzer, "probably about twelve miles."

"Okay. That could be. And if we drive at the speed limit, how long do you think it will be before we reach the Soo?"

"Which Soo do you mean," I asked, "the Michigan Soo or the Ontario Soo? Because I don't know how often you've crossed the border up here, but you just never know how it's going to go. You can't predict how long the line of cars and trucks on the bridge will be, and you don't know whether customs is going to rummage through your gear."

"No, I wasn't thinking about all that," Tommy said. "I wondered how long you think it will take us to get from here to the Michigan Soo if we drive the speed limit."

"I don't know for sure," I said, "probably about an hour and a half. Maybe closer to two hours. Wait a second. What are you doing? You're sitting back there with a GPS, aren't you? That's why you're asking all these questions. You're checking everything out with a GPS."

"I just got it for my birthday. It's awesome!"

"Awesome? It sounds like trouble to me," I said. "That's what it is — big trouble."

"How could it be trouble?" Tommy said. "It's been right about everything I've checked so far."

"Well, maybe I've got a good idea about what you're planning to do once we get to Eagle Lake. You and Joel are going to hop in a boat and think you can find your way around just because you can check that little screen. But you'll probably end up getting turned around and confused somewhere and won't have a clue about how to get back to the camp. Do you have any idea how much trouble that's going to cause Joel? That's exactly the kind of thing that would set him off."

"We're not gonna get lost. How could we? Last week Joel showed me the map of Eagle that he has, and it has a bunch of GPS reference points with their coordinates. I'll punch those in, and then we'll be able to go wherever we want."

"Not in our lifetime!" I said, my voice rising. "I've spent plenty of time studying that map, and if one thing jumps out at me, it's that Eagle is big and complicated. The bay that our camp sits on is wide open. But just outside that bay things start to get really confusing. Did you see all those islands and navigational hazards on the map? They're the little red asterisks. Plus, there's all kinds of jagged peninsulas and narrow channels. It looks like a big watery maze to me."

"Okay, but it says on the directions that this unit is accurate to within twenty-nine feet."

"Twenty-nine feet! Twenty-nine feet! You obviously haven't been on any Canadian Shield lake before. In plenty of places you can have really deep water and then twenty-nine feet one side or the other will be boulders the size of freight cars. And just because you can punch in coordinates for reference points on the map, that doesn't guarantee that you can cruise from one of those spots to another without running up on something. You've got to know things about lake structure and the color of water in the distance if you're going to make it from point to point without a terrible accident."

"But Joel's been to Canada before. With what he knows about reading water, plus the map and my GPS, we'll figure things out."

"Tommy, you've got to promise me something, and you've got to promise right now, while Joel is still sleeping: You've got to promise that you and Joel won't head off and get yourselves lost. You understand that? You sure? Do you promise?"

"Joel and I will only go to those places that we're sure we can find our way back from. I promise. The two of us always know where in the world we are."

The next day, by the time we had driven from our hotel in Thunder Bay to the camp on Eagle Lake, and after we had unloaded the van, rigged up our rods, and filled out the form for our fishing licenses, we had about two hours to get out on the water.

As I came down to the dock, Duzzer was already set up in the bow of our boat waiting for me to get going. I dawdled a bit, arranging and storing my gear, mainly so that I could check where Joel and T-Gunz were heading off in their boat. To my relief, they motored straight across the bay from our camp and then used the trolling motor to position themselves a short distance outside an extensive stretch of pencil reeds. And they stayed just off those reeds the whole night. I know because I took Duzzer along the eastern ends of two islands just off the mouth of our bay, and I could check on Joel and T-Gunz's location with seemingly casual glances over one shoulder or the other.

When we were all back at the dock at twilight, I waited to check on Joel until he was alone in his boat, untangling some of the lures he had tossed together in a compartment.

"Well?"

"Well, what?"

"Anything?"

"Yeah, we saw two big ones, but we couldn't get them to eat. Pretty lazy follows, both of them."

"I don't mean that. Did you have any trouble? Any anxiety? Like last summer?"

"No. No. Come to think of it, I didn't have a bit of trouble. T-Gunz is so funny while he fishes that I hardly stopped laughing long enough to start thinking about myself."

"He is?"

"Yeah, sometime this week you've got to go out with him and watch him retrieve a jerkbait. He uses what he calls a zigzag method. He casts and then starts the retrieve with his rod tip low, just above the water, and way to his left. Then as he's reeling he suddenly whips his rod off to the right. Then back to the left. Then right again. He whips that lure back and forth so hard I'm surprised he doesn't tear the line guides off his rod."

"No way he's going to catch a musky fooling around like that," I said.

"I wouldn't be so sure. He caught a decent pike already tonight. We found some heavy cabbage fifteen yards or so outside those reeds across there, and I called two big muskies out —

probably mid-to-high-forties fish. Just a few seconds after the second follow, T. hooked a pike. You should have seen him. 'What do I do, Joel? What do I do?' At one point he got so excited I thought he almost lost his grip on his rod. But I helped him play that fish out. I didn't want to waste time netting a pike since we're after muskies, so I told him to try to shake it off his line. But it was his first fish ever, he said, and he wanted me to net it. He wanted a picture. As soon as I scooped it up, he went nuts. 'Yahtzee!' he yells out, 'Yahtzee!' and starts sprinting in place in the boat. But then he was afraid to touch his own fish — I think he could see some of the slime that had rubbed off on the net. So I had to hold the pike while T. propped his camera on my tackle box, set the timer, and then hustled back and stood next to me. I was laughing so hard I got the hiccups for a while."

"Hope that picture turns out," I said. "Did you see it already? Yeah? So his camera is a digital — that figures. But before that, you called up two nice muskies?"

"Yeah. Like I said, they were lazy follows, but they were nice fish, really nice fish. And now I know where they hang out."

"That is great! That is just so great that you found some big muskies right out across the bay from our camp. Duzzer and I went farther out, around those two islands just beyond the mouth, and didn't see a thing. If you guys put some serious time into those fish this week, I'm sure you'll nail one of them sooner or later. Maybe both."

"Oh, we'll find some time for those fish this week," he said, "no doubt about that."

∞

After I had rolled out of bed the next morning and had done the stretches I use to fight the arthritis in my left hip, I found Jon, Jason, and Duzzer passing a box of Honey-Nut Cheerios around the kitchen table and pointing to various islands and shoals on a spread-out map of Eagle.

"Joel and T-Gunz still in bed?" I wondered aloud.

"Morning to you, too," said Duzzer.

"Joel and T-Gunz?" Jason said. "They got up really early, packed some pop and snacks, and headed down to the dock. They said they had some exploring to do."

"Where? Did they say where they were going? Or did they leave some kind of note?"

"That's all they said," Jason said. "They took Joel's map, and T-Gunz has a new GPS. Did you know he has a GPS? I guess he punched in a bunch of coordinates last night before they fell asleep. I gotta buy one of those. With a GPS I could make it all the way down to Coleman's Reef, and I hear that's where the biggest ladies in the lake hang out."

"Maybe they stayed in our bay," I said, almost praying the words. I hustled out to our front deck and looked across to where the two boys had fished the night before. No boat. Nothing up in the mouth of the bay either, out toward where Duzzer and I had been last night.

I went back inside and started to pace, stepping over boots and tackle boxes as I went.

"Now what do we do?" I asked. "I knew this would happen. I just knew this would happen. Tommy thinks he can find his way around in the wild with that little gizmo, but the wildest place he's ever known is the field behind your school. Those two are going to get lost or run their boat up on some shoal, and then Joel will be so scared he won't know what to do. He won't be able to fight it off. He'll lose it. I just know he'll lose it, and I won't be anywhere around to help him. I thought I was clear with Tommy about how much trouble that GPS could be. Wonder what we can do. Maybe I should tell the head dockboy about this and see if he can free up a couple of guys to help us search for those guys."

"Hold on a second!" Duzzer's tone was stern. "We didn't come all the way up here just so that some of us could fly around looking for the others. We're here to fish, and fish is what we're going to do. We'll probably want to keep moving out away from our bay here, and we'll keep our eyes open for Joel and T-Gunz, but we're going to fish as we head farther and farther out. Joel knows what he's doing when he's on the water. You know that. In the past I've seen him set you straight once or twice when you got disoriented. And T-Gunz is like some kind of electronics wizard. Plus, you can't forget that he promised you not to go anyplace he couldn't find his way back from. So let's load up and get out there and see if any big ones are interested. If we see those two guys along the way somewhere, fine. If not, they'll be back here at suppertime."

I have had some awful days on fishing trips. Once I came down with a strain of intestinal flu while Duzzer and I were on a trip to Little Bay de Noc for walleye, and I got so weak, I remember, that after crawling to the toilet in our rented cabin and being racked by the dry heaves, I had to lie on the floor of the bathroom for twenty minutes — maybe thirty minutes — until I could find the energy to crawl back to bed. Another time up north, I had to take Jason to a small local emergency room — one nurse and one doctor attending — and watch while a young M.D. took a scalpel and sliced deep and then deeper in order to get a clamp on the hook that a thrashing fish had buried in Jason's thumb.

But that day on Eagle Lake was the worst. Duzzer and I were in one boat, and Jon and Jason in another, as we did what Duzzer had said we should do. We motored out to the mouth of our bay, and then two of us picked one island to fish around while the other two picked another. When we had fished one pair of islands, we moved west and picked out two more. The shores of the islands had numerous shelves of rock sheering away into the water. They had extensive beds of cabbage outside them, often extending into twelve or thirteen feet of water. And occasionally we could see jumbled boulders below the surface in eight or ten feet of water. Much of the territory could have held muskies.

But I couldn't concentrate. I spent more time scanning the horizon than watching the water behind my lure. *Where can those two guys be?* I kept wondering. *How is Joel doing? Oh God, please keep Joel safe. Keep him calm. Keep him from panic.* I was so distracted that I missed two follows. Duzzer, who usually spotted follows only after I did, hissed at me just in time for me to see shadowy forms turning away. When Jon and Jason came over to tell us about the beautiful forty-inch tiger musky that Jason had hooked on an L-turn and then landed, I missed most of the details.

I wished that day of my life away. *Maybe they'll be back at the dock before us,* I wished. *Maybe they'll be back already when we pull up. Please, please, please.* But when we returned for supper, their mooring spot was still empty.

"Well," Duzzer suggested, "you could haul a chair out here

on the dock and keep watch for them while I get supper started. You'll be able to see them when they enter the bay."

"I couldn't stand that. I'd fidget myself right off the dock. I gotta do something. Gotta move. I'm gonna take a walk down the road into camp. Oh, if those two guys —"

"Just go!" he said, waving toward shore. "Take your walk. I'll start supper, and maybe Jon will help me. It looks like Jase is going to take some casts from that outer dock. When you come back, I'll bet you anything those guys'll be back."

I trudged up the hill toward the road. I had heard people say that they had seen mink and even moose along the mile-long two-track connecting the camp to a gravel road leading west toward Vermillion Bay. But as I walked I was unable to focus outside my own skin. Why was there so much throbbing in my left temple? So steadily in such a small spot? *I've had nothing like this ever before,* I thought. *Feels like something's going to erupt out of my head. What do my speech-pathology students say? "How bad is the pain?" If stroke victims can talk, what do they say? Not a stroke — please, not a stroke. Especially not on the left side. So much of what I live for is controlled on the left. Is there a hospital around here? Dryden. Probably one in Dryden. Maybe not a big one, but still a hospital. Will they have people trained to treat strokes? Probably have to send me to Thunder Bay.*

That one time when I had to bring Joel to the emergency room for stitches on his knee — that woman on the bed in the hallway. Lying on her side facing the wall, gibbering to herself. "A small stroke, and someone is coming to take her upstairs," the nurses said. *Had she made it? If she had died there, how long before anyone noticed?*

Then some scuffing, some scuffing of gravel behind me. I whirled, fiery pinpricks sweeping across my scalp.

It was Joel, with T-Gunz's digital camera around his neck.

"You're back?"

"Yup. Where'd you think we'd be? We pulled up at the dock about ten minutes after you left. They told me you headed out this way, and I said I'd go find you. Duzzer's got supper started. If we eat quick, we can get back out there tonight. Maybe get another one."

"Another?"

"We got a nice one today, Dad, a really nice one. Here, look." He dialed up a picture on the screen of T-Gunz's camera and handed the camera to me. Just to the left of center stood Joel, who was holding a good muskie horizontally, and just to the left of Joel, with one arm around Joel's shoulders and the other high in the air in a victory flourish, stood T-Gunz. Both were grinning as broadly as I had ever seen.

"Gorgeous. That's a gorgeous fish, Joel. How big was it?"

"Forty-seven inches on the nose. And a twenty-four-inch girth. Did you see its head? Its head is humungous. That fish is going to grow up to be a real monster someday."

"What'd you get it on?"

"I didn't get it — T. did."

"T-Gunz? No way. I know he's a fast learner, but he hasn't had enough experience to land a fish like that. For most people, that's the fish of a lifetime. My biggest so far is only forty-four inches, and I almost lost that one. No way T-Gunz could land a fish like that."

"Well, he did. We found this great little spot. A channel between the mainland and an island. Pencil reeds along both sides of the channel. But pretty deep water — twelve or fifteen feet — in the middle of the channel. And just where the channel opens up to the south, a huge boulder, a boulder practically the size of our van, on the island side of the channel. When we first cast outside that boulder, I called this muskie up. It started out eight or ten feet behind my bucktail, but then it really closed and I thought for sure it was going to hit, but it just kept following, right through my L-turn and then around as I did some figure eights. You shoulda seen it — it was right on the bucktail. I even brushed the fish's snoot once or twice with the skirt. And I was whispering to it, 'C'mon, baby, eat my lure, just eat it.' It never hit, not even a little nip. But when we stopped back in that spot on our way back to camp, T. tosses out his silver Funky Chicken, and as I'm putting the trolling motor down, I hear him say, 'There's one.'"

"He hooked it on his first cast when you stopped back?"

"Yup. Just flipped that spinner out and the fish took it. He told me later that the spinner hit the water and just stopped. We came close to losing that fish about a dozen different ways. The worst was when the fish tried to wrap the line around the prop, but I leaned way over, grabbed the line, and guided it around and to the left. Then as I was lifting the motor out of the water, the fish jumped and almost dislodged the lure on the side of the boat. But the hook held and T. held on. I helped him with his drag, and we finally got that beast in the net. Then we did the old prop-the-camera-on-the-tackle-box trick and set the timer and got some pictures. Hit that review button. On the right there. We got about six pictures in all."

"Hold on. Weren't you just a little bit ticked off?"

"Ticked off? Why ticked off?"

"Well, you called that fish up in the first place. Once you guys went back, he probably should've kept his lure in the boat until you had a good crack at it. Instead, he just goes right ahead and casts in front of you. I think I'd be ticked."

"That's not the way we roll, Dad. Plus, it was great to see how excited he was. Not right away. Not while I was unhooking the fish and holding it and he was setting his camera up. Not even as we were posing for the shots. But as soon as we got it back in the water and it swam off, it was like T. had some kind of injection. He was dancing around the boat yelling, 'Yahtzee, yahtzee, yahtzee!' Then he had to sit down, his legs were shaking so much."

"Okay, so where's this spot? Where were you when all this happened? I was keeping an eye out for you guys the whole day, and I didn't spot you once."

"We started out by going down the Backchannel a ways."

"The Backchannel? Where's that? I've never heard of any Backchannel."

"You pick it up down and across from what's called Canoe Narrows. You should see the channel, Dad. It's got a lot of sheer rock faces falling straight into the water. Mostly pinkish orange rock with creamy veins in it. We went on down that channel, and that great spot where we got the muskie was back in a huge bay I think T. said was called El Dorado."

"Goodness gracious, Joel! I remember seeing El Dorado on the map. That bay's got to be at least fifteen miles from camp. At least the mouth of it is. If you went all the way down into the back of it, you were probably eighteen miles from camp. How in the world did you manage that? I can't believe it. Weren't you freaking out — absolutely freaking out?"

"Nope. T.'s so good with his GPS and the map that we never wondered where we were. Or what direction we were headed in. North, south, east, or west — T. had it all straight. Plus, on the way down to El Dorado, we stopped at a ton of good-looking spots and made a few casts. We must have found close to a hundred that looked good enough to be worth some serious exploration."

"Closed to a hundred? You've got to be kidding. Don't you remember how long it takes to fish a single spot really thoroughly? Or how many days we have left up here?"

"I know all that," Joel said. "But you weren't planning to make just one trip way up here, were you?" ⑥

Dock Boy

Only a few minutes after the robins and phoebes had begun their prebreakfast themes with minimal variations, Jason had wrestled his way out of his sleeping bag in the loft of our rented cabin, groped around until he found his clothes and flip-flops, clumped his way down the steep and narrow set of stairs, and grabbed a chocolate-chip cookie and a can of Mountain Dew for breakfast. Then he had left a clear trail in the dew on his way down to the dock. But now he was back outside our front door, his nose indenting the screen.

"But Mom, why did you say I had to wear a life jacket if I go out on the dock? Our life jackets are so tight they practically choke me. There's a bunch of other kids down there, they're not much older than me, and not a single one has a life jacket on. And besides, all of our jackets are those clumpy old orange ones. They have those straps that nobody knows what to do with. Jon and Joel say I'm supposed to bring those straps from the back, run them between my legs, and tie them in the front. Who wears that kind of life jacket anymore? What am I supposed to do — spend my whole vacation looking like a dork from the Lower Peninsula?"

"Well, no matter how old our preservers are, and no matter

what they look like, maybe it's because you're only five years old and I know you won't watch where you put your feet when you race around fishing. That dock, I noticed on our little tour last night, has boards sticking up all over the place, and the water you'll land in when you trip and fall is way over your head and you've only finished tadpole swimming lessons so far. Or if you don't think that makes sense, just say it's because we love you."

It was our family's first morning at a resort on Snows Channel in the Les Cheneaux Islands, a resort with nine ancient cabins and one new one, a beach-volleyball court, two horseshoe pits, a small swimming beach with detergent bottles anchored offshore serving as boundary markers, a screened-in fish-cleaning house, and a dock.

When most people hear the word *dock*, they think of structures associated with decades-old cottages on small inland lakes, uneven and shaky wooden or aluminum walkways a few feet wide and about fifteen feet long, with support poles resting on squares of plywood stacked in the muck or sand on the lake bottom. Many of these have a rowboat or paddleboat tethered against old tires hung over the support poles.

The dock at our resort was nothing like that. It was about six feet wide and started with a set of three steps on the sand of the shore, ran west into Snows Channel for about thirty-five yards, and then made a ninety-degree left turn and extended to the south for another eight or ten yards. If you were able to view just this main section of the dock from the air, it would resemble a capital L with a base perhaps not quite in the conventional proportion to the vertical segment. But before the dock got all the way out to this base, it had a boathouse built off its south side, a boathouse with enough boat slips to moor six boats out of the weather, and each of these boat slips had its own finger dock. Starting near the deep-water edge of that boathouse, but on the other side of the dock, was a walkway that extended ten or twelve yards to the north and then made a left turn and led into the doorway of a second, smaller boathouse, this one reserved for the resort owner's vintage Chris Craft and a collection of old lures stuck in corkboard on the walls. All parts of this dock — the support posts and planking — were cedar, and the primary supports were anchored in footings of limestone blocks piled within rectangular boxes of joined logs, also cedar. I have driven through rural villages that seemed smaller than the dock at our resort.

Jason must have assumed that the eastern Upper Peninsula offered nothing better for vacationers to do than fish from this dock, because it was the first place he went every morning and the place we had to call him away from every night. He would trot from spot to spot out there, stopping every so often to make a cast with his fiberglass rod, leaning against a support pole while waiting to see if his offering, perhaps a jig and night crawler or minnow, had attracted some fish's attention. He was out there so consistently that I, wherever I happened to be and whatever I happened to be doing — reading with Wanda on the beach, serving a volleyball to Jon or Joel, trying to make a horseshoe spin just the right number of times before opening up and curling around the stake, or trolling just inside the green buoys in the channel south of our resort — expected to be able to turn toward our dock, focus, and locate Jason's distinct spot of orange among all the other colorful small shapes out there.

More than once that week I tried to persuade him to come

out in the boat with some of the rest of us: "Come on, Jase. It's fine if you get up before the rest of us and spend some time on the dock. I bet you'll catch a mess of rock bass and perch. But a boat comes with the cottage, and there are lots of spots in the channel and the bays that you should try. You should see the beautiful cabbage out by Buoy 10. The boulders and drop-offs around what your brothers have named 'Jackpot Point' look perfect. And I hear there could be spawning smallmouth in Peck Bay, out toward the end of the middle passage, bigger small-mouth than any we have back home."

But his mind was fixed: he was competing with the other kids on the dock during that week for catch-and-release suprem-acy, and he didn't want to fall behind in the competition by be-ing in the boat. For the first few days of our week, I gave in and let him spend his fourteen or fifteen hours each day exploring and re-exploring the waters around the dock. After all, I figured, sometimes Wanda and always Jon and Joel were eager to go out with me in the boat. Once we were on the water, they kept me busy enough with knot tying and lure selection and boat posi-tioning. Plus, I was still learning what spots in the channels and bays were productive. It's true that the perch and rock bass that Jason caught from our dock were all pretty small, but for the first few days of our vacation those fish clearly outnumbered the handful of pike that the rest of us caught while out in the boat.

But on Wednesday morning I took Jon and Joel trolling south around the tip of our peninsula and then northeast to-ward Cedarville, and in an extensive bed of cabbage in front of a boathouse whose roof was covered with waves of guano, we found a pack of hungry pike. We were trolling blue and silver Rattletraps, partly because they resembled herring but mainly because they didn't get fouled up in the cabbage too often. Almost every time we made a trolling pass, especially whenever one of the boys felt his Rattletrap hit the stalk or leaf of a weed and would snap it off, a pike would hit: a slashing strike usually from the side as the pike would turn on the bait, then weightlessness on the line as the fish came toward us fast, a frenzy alongside us as the pike saw the boat and tried to take the line deep and wrap it around the base of cabbage stalks, and finally our victory celebration after the boys would scream, "Get it, Dad — get it in the net!"

"You've got to get its head up," I would hiss back. "I can't take it from this angle. It'll flip out. Get its head up and lead it this way! Okay, there you go, that's right, a little more, a little more — she's going to be yours, and now she is. Baby, baby, baby! We should have had a film crew here for that fight!"

After Jon and Joel had each caught five pike, all thirty inches or longer, I thought of Jason catching five-inch perch on our dock.

"That's about as much action as you guys have had at any one time in your lives. That's more action than some guys ever have on an outing. We've got to go back and get Jase. Something's keeping the pike in this weed bed — probably a bunch of baitfish — even after all the fights and commotion we've had, so they'll probably still be here once we pick him up and come back. I've got to give him a chance to fight fish bigger than he'll catch on the dock."

"Aw, Dad, that dock is his whole world right now," Jon said. "Why don't we just leave him alone? You know he's about as happy as a five-year-old can get. He's always liked it when there's nobody around to tell him how to fish."

"Yeah," Joel agreed, "and it's not always so pretty when all three of us boys fish with you. Remember that time you took us all to Myers Lake and we discovered those frogs? You weren't too happy that day. For a while after that, you wouldn't even take the three of us fishing at the same time."

"True," I nodded, "but there's something electric out here. You can just feel it. This is one of those days you're lucky to see every few years. I've got to give him a chance at it, too." I fired up the engine and started back around the point and up the channel to our resort.

It took us about ten minutes to get back to the dock, and Jon and Joel approached it with the callow arrogance of self-proclaimed heroes, standing up in the boat, waving their T-shirts around their heads, flexing their biceps and posing.

"Jase," Jon called out as we glided toward the outermost section of the dock, "get over here. It's important!"

"I'm busy," Jason said.

"Get over here right now or I'll come over there and throw you in!"

"Okay, okay, so what is it?" he asked as he trotted over. "What's the big deal? I'm right in the middle of something. Petey just found a Christmas tree sunk under one of the finger docks in the boathouse, and there's a bunch of perch around it. If I stay out here too long, that curly-haired little dude from Cabin Six is going to catch up to me. What do you want?"

"Not so lippy!" Joel snapped. "We did you a big favor coming all the way back here. Down around the end of the peninsula we found a mess of weeds all over in front of an old boathouse, and pike are all through the weeds. Jon and I have both caught five all by ourselves — Dad didn't even have to help too much. Big. Thirty inches plus. Thirty-five inchers. And I lost one that had to be even bigger than that. A huge greenish-brown back. Dad thinks those pike are going to stay in the weeds. So we're giving you the chance to come out with us now and catch some real fish, not those little squeakers you've been messing with. Six-inch perch — why don't you get real?"

"Six-inch perch — you'd better believe it!" Jason shot back. "Five fish for each of you? I hope you didn't say 'five fish.' I caught five fish before you were even down past that first buoy this morning. And I'm up to thirty-seven for the morning, three hundred and six for the week. And there are big fish around here too, bigger than anything you're ever going to see."

"What do you mean — big fish? You feeding us a story?" I said.

"No way! Just this morning, after you guys were out of sight down the channel, that man from the half-painted cabin by the driveway, the guy who wears those gross plaid shorts, hauls a plastic chair out to the corner of the dock over there. He snaps a night crawler harness on his line, hooks a crawler in a couple of places, messes with his reel a little, and finally lobs the bait out across the channel toward the island. On his first cast, his first cast I tell you, he says he feels like he pulled it into a stump. His line just stops. He's so surprised that a stump would be right out in the middle of the boating channel that he's not sure what to do. He's just sitting there holding a tight line. Then he asks some of us kids if we'll hop in a boat and row out and see if we can pull his crawler harness out from the back side.

"But you know what happens then? The guy can't believe it, and we can't either. Nobody can believe it. His line starts moving. It's almost creepy. No swirls in the water. No jumps. No big runs. His line just moves slow and steady. First toward the dock. Then along the outside edge of the dock out here, around the corner and in toward shore. The guy has to get up and follow his line. Every once in a while he has to raise his rod over a support pole. Then the fish turns and heads back, comes around the corner again, and swims along the outside edge headed in the other direction. Still really slow and steady. And we never see it. Whatever it is, it's like it doesn't even know it's hooked. Or if it does know, it acts like it's no big deal. And the guy is standing out here and he gets so excited he can't even talk normal. 'Get a big net,' he's screaming at us, 'get a big net out here right now!' So we run back into the owner's boathouse and scrounge around and find this gigantic net — it's so big I could net a paddleboat with it — and when we get it out to the end of the dock, the guy says, 'Good, now I'm going to show this fish who's boss — I didn't drive all the way from Rochester Hills to let a fish get the better of me.'

"He's doing everything wrong. He's leaning back, jerking on the line and horsing that fish, and when it turns away toward the far side of the channel he tightens his drag as far as it will go and horses on that fish some more. And then there's this sharp 'bwink' and his line snaps and settles in a bunch of loops on the water, and the guy starts swearing all over the place. Good thing Mom wasn't out here then.

"Afterwards I asked the resort owner what he thought that fish must have been, and he said it almost had to be a musky, a Great Lakes musky. Just last week, he said, a kid about my age hooked a four-footer from a dock down the channel and two guys trolling past stopped, reeled up their lines, watched the fight for a while, and then rowed over and netted the fish for him. The guy on our dock should never have lost that fish. It was almost a crime — if he had just taken a little time, he would have caught what had to be the biggest fish of just about anybody's life. So you can have all the pike you want. I'm going to stay here. I might catch a lot of little ones, but sooner or later I'm going to hook a musky. That one should have bit on my line in the first place. I would have landed it, even if it took a while. I've even switched to a heavier jig."

"That was pretty good!" Joel said. "Ever think about telling stories for a living?"

"He's getting quite the imagination," Jon whispered to me.

"True," I agreed, "but I don't want to call him a liar and start a big scene out here right now. Let's just leave him and head back to our cabbage bed."

When we got back, though, two other boats had anchored in the path of our trolling run, and we decided to move on and check out the marina in Cedarville. But even after we had come back to the cabin for lunch, and for most of the other days of our vacation, we couldn't talk Jason off that dock. We found several other spots — a deep rock bar guarding the mouth of the middle passage, a slot between two boulders on the backside of an island northwest toward Hessel, and a weed flat in the channel leading into Peck Bay, where we could usually pick up a decent-sized pike or two and occasionally a smallmouth. And Jason ended up winning the week's competition on the dock by catching 736 fish — all perch and rock bass. No one, he said, hooked into that musky again. "If only I could have had a little more time on the dock," he repeated on the drive home.

In the weeks after we got back to Grand Rapids that summer, my time spent fishing with Jason forced me to admit that all of his activity on that dock up north had made him a markedly better fisherman. For one thing, his time on the dock had taught him to fish very tight to structure. He had seen perch hiding among the denuded branches of submerged Christmas trees, rock bass lying in the small open spaces within cinder blocks wedged among chunks of limestone, and even a small pike hiding inside a submerged tire. So whenever he and I fished a flat with a spread of tree stumps, he would clang spinnerbaits right off the stumps before letting them fall into the water and starting to retrieve them. When we fished lakes with large trees blown over along the shore, their tops extending well out past the drop-off, Jason flipped spoons right into the tight little crotches where branches intersected the trunk. When we fished lakes with a thick outside weed edge, he would toss a Texas-rigged lizard right onto the weeds, lift his rod, jiggle the bait, and let it fall on the outside of the weeds, its tail twirling. When we fished lakes with pontoon boats moored with their bows toward shore, he pestered me to position him directly off the stern of the boat so that he could flip a tube bait past the pontoons' engines into the shaded waters below.

True, he caught lots of fish that way, more than I did with my stewardly casts a couple of feet shy of possible snags. But he was not always perfectly accurate, and more than once on every occasion he and I were on the water together, I would have to take a really deep breath and turn when I'd hear him say, "Oops — snagged again. Can you take me over to that dock? I'm wrapped around the gas line of that pontoon." I was never the happiest person on the lake at those times, and he knew it. But all he ever said after I'd helped him retrieve his snagged lure was, "Just remember, Dad, you can't be afraid to go where the big fish are!" I never replied, but I knew he was right.

Another way all that time on the dock on Snows Channel had made him a better angler was that it had led him to be fascinated by lures. When he was on that dock, if one little kid caught a fish, no matter how big it was, all the other kids would swarm around him, pestering the successful angler with questions about what bait or lure he had used. Plus, throughout the day, groups of anglers would come out to the dock, get in their boats, and head out for a while, and on their return, all those kids would leave their fishing for a few minutes and throw question after question the anglers' way about what they had caught and what lures they had used. And when all the boats were safely moored each night, those same little kids would walk up and down the finger docks and look with envy at all the lures that had been left hanging on rods and tossed into storage spaces. After that week, Jason would often ask me to take him to sporting-goods stores just so that he could check out various lures.

His fascination with lures in general was closely related to the fact that during the rest of that summer, over the course of a normal fishing excursion, Jason would do more productive experimenting with lure retrieves than anyone else I have ever fished with. On the dock up at Les Cheneaux, he and his competitors often targeted fish they could see — a ten-inch perch, say, holding tight to one of the cedar pilings of the dock. Fish like that would see many lures worked in many different ways throughout a day. At some point, Jason had obviously learned that he had to try something different with fish that were so wise to baits, and perhaps even weary of them, that he had to work lures in new and enticing ways. His winning of the contest that first year on the dock was testimony to his inventiveness — inventiveness that was right on the edge of being zany.

I got used to being startled when he fished with me that summer. Once when he and I waded some sections of the Flat River, when the water was so low that it never even reached his thighs, he tried something that I'm sure would have been risky had he been using lighter line. He was casting a Baby One-minus, and at one point he took the line directly above the swivel and looped it around one of the front treble hooks. That lure had a very pronounced wobble without the looped line; with it, the lure both wobbled and turned over on itself. If I had been a fish, I would have found his offering laughable, maybe even insulting to my intelligence. But the smallmouth, at least the Flat River smallmouth that day, could not let the lure pass them by. They hammered it, sometimes two or three from different angles at the same time.

On another outing that summer, Duzzer, Jason, and I were using Pop R's for largemouth bass in Lake Monterey at Sandy Pines. Duzzer and I were giving our lures frequent and almost violent jerks. We liked the sound our lures made: *Baloop! Baloop! Baloop!* We were working those lures the only way we had ever seen them worked. But Jason tried something different: he gave his Pop R infrequent and ever-so-slight twitches with his rod tip, so that his lure made delicate little disturbances of the water's surface: plip, an agonizingly long wait, another plip, another long wait, then another plip. I didn't think the largemouth could even notice what he was doing with his lure. But that night he outfished both Duzzer and me, the stubborn old guys who refused to follow his lead, at least three to one. At one point Duzzer gave me a miffed look and whispered: "This kid has figured out how to get inside a fish's head!"

Toward the end of that summer, he went beyond experimenting with how to retrieve conventional lures in new ways: he started building his own baits. The first one that I remember seeing was so grotesque that I could not imagine it fooling a fish. He called it The Octopus. He took eight large curly tails and threaded them one by one on a large jig. When he cast it out and retrieved it slowly, with an occasional jerk on the line, it looked like a modern Medusa in the water.

"It's going to scare away everything within a half mile of here — or turn it to stone," I said.

"But don't you think it looks like an octopus or maybe even some kind of juicy jellyfish?"

"Maybe it does, but how many fish in Gun Lake ever see an octopus or jellyfish? Maybe you should attach a little note to your line explaining that this creation is edible!"

His second homemade lure actually caught him some pike, especially on overcast days on Muskegon Lake. This one he called The Sweep. He sawed about six inches off a yellow broom handle, filed a mouth-like slot in the leading edge, attached two sets of eye hooks and treble hooks to the bottom, and tossed it over weed beds. He would let it sit for a few seconds, then give it a sharp jerk, then wait a second, then give it another jerk, and so on, always trying to keep his line taut. More than once when I was with him, just as he was ready to jerk it once more, he would feel the weight of a pike on his line and set the hook.

Even if one of his homemade lures did not produce for him right away, he never lost faith in it. When his brothers were using spoons or spinnerbaits to haul pike out of weedbeds and were urging Jason to switch from his own jerkbait with a propeller twirling on its hind end — a bait attracting no attention from fish whatsoever — he would invariably respond to them with something like, "What's the big rush? This lure, like all my lures, has a lifetime guarantee on it, which means that at some point in my lifetime, as long as I fish it with confidence, I'm guaranteed to catch a big fish with it!"

Even though I had to acknowledge more than once that the Snows Channel dock had helped Jason become a better angler, when the boys started asking during the following winter where our next summer fishing trip would be, and I finally decided we should travel a bit farther and try Little Bay de Noc, I also decided that I would have to force Jason to spend most of his time not on a new dock but out in the boat with the rest of us. After all, I told myself, if he spent a week on a dock on the Little Bay, he would miss all kinds of good fishing spots, spots that were famous in U.P. angling lore. He would miss trolling in front of the river mouths for walleye, casting into the large weed beds south of Escanaba for monster pike, and probing the rock ledges on the east side of the bay for smallmouth. Furthermore, what sense did it make for him to spend so much of a family vacation apart from his family? I was prepared, if he resisted, to have him stay back in Grand Rapids with his aunt and uncle (I figured he probably wasn't old enough to catch the contradiction in my reasoning). Sometimes fathers have to make hard decisions and stick with them, and I was the father.

When I told him what I had decided, he only gave a dry sniff and stared at me. Or no, maybe he was staring at some point behind me and to my left.

But I needed to know that he had heard me: "You get it?" I asked.

"Not really. Do parents have the right to tell their kids to kill their dreams? You don't think it's possible for me to catch the fish of my life from a dock, do you?"

"Well, maybe, maybe not, but for the week of our summer vacation, I want most of us together most of the time. If you want to fight me on this, you can stay behind. Aunt Barb says you can stay at their place."

His head snapped up: "You'd leave me behind? Jon and Joel could go, but I couldn't? No way! You can't just leave me. I can't believe this! I'm probably the best fisherman in the whole family, and it's a fishing vacation, so I have to go."

It's been several years now since that confrontation, years that have seen us traveling to fishing camps throughout northern Michigan and even, as the boys grew older, into Ontario. Every place after Les Cheneaux, Jason didn't fight me and spent most of each day out in the boat with two or three or four of the rest of us. And especially as he grew into his middle teens, it became very difficult for any of the rest of us to outfish him. He would often beat us in both numbers and sizes. But at every one of these camps, even as he abandoned most of his boyish ways (and Wanda and I would usually forget to make him wear a life jacket), he showed an unwavering fascination with docks.

Some years ago we spent a week at a resort south of Chapleau, Ontario. To hear Jason tell it, the best feature of this resort was clearly its large T-shaped dock, a dock that had once served as the mooring place for a floatplane. Whenever we had time back in camp, Jason spent it on this dock. He would get up before the rest of us, be the last to arrive for meals and the most insistent that we hurry through them, and stay out long after dark, when Jon and Joel would be relaxing on their beds looking at pictures of frighteningly large fish in copies of Musky Hunter magazine.

From the top part of the T, Jason cast buzzbaits to stretches of pencil reeds that lay on either side of the channel leading away from the dock, reeds that were inhabited by numerous pike. He told us that he could usually see an expanding V in the water, sometimes even a fin and a tail, as a pike would come up on his buzzbait. Though many of those pike, once hooked, would shake off his lure in the reeds, those noisy fights were all that Jason talked about after we got home.

The following winter, the boys used the Internet to learn about a resort that was most of the way around Lake Superior and then northwest of Thunder Bay. Online testimonials said that this camp offered the best combination of musky and smallmouth fishing anywhere in northwest Ontario. Since we believe most of what we ever read about fishing, we didn't need to do any more research. However, an hour or so after we got there on a Saturday late in June, while Wanda and I were still sorting out supplies in the cabin, Jason returned from the dock looking devastated.

"Alan, the owner, says I can't fish from the dock," he reported. " 'Too dangerous for the other guests,' he says. What's the deal? Does he think I don't know where I'm casting? I'm not going to hook anybody. Why did we ever pick this place anyway? Is it too late to move somewhere else?"

He moped for a while, but it didn't take him long to come up with a response as mischievous as it was creative. When we weren't using the two boats that were reserved for us, usually because the local birds hadn't yet roused us, Jason would step into one of the boats, untie and push off, row eight or ten feet away from the dock, and then skip tube baits under the moored boats and various sections of the dock for the smallmouth that were lying in the shade. The resort owner clearly wasn't pleased to have this adolescent playing — and winning — physical and mental games with him, but the posted rule was that no fishing was allowed from the dock, and even the camp dog could see that Jason wasn't on the dock.

Through the years, Jason's adventures on docks haven't come without his paying various kinds of prices. Since he is usually the last one to come in for meals, he often does not get his fair share of the treats that Wanda sometimes surprises us with. We would call everyone to the table, where Wanda had laid out some fresh cinnamon rolls she had found in a bakery in Cedarville, Chapleau, or Sioux Lookout. Jon, Joel, Wanda, and I would all be sitting in the kitchen waiting for Jason and looking covetously at the cinnamon rolls.

"Where is he? Did you call him?" Wanda would ask.

"I did! I went all the way over to the edge of the main drive and called him."

"How long ago was that? Did he answer? Did he say he was coming?"

"Sure, he answered. Same as always — 'Right away, Dad, I'll be there in a second. Just one more cast.'"

"So where is he, then? That's a pretty long second."

"I don't know. You want me to go back down to the dock and see what he's up to?"

While Wanda and I were preoccupied with this discussion, of course, Jon and Joel had cut off and eaten more than their share of the cinnamon rolls. When Jason finally banged the door open — "Oh, you started already? I just had one more place to try" — he wouldn't have had a fragment of cinnamon roll at all if Wanda and I hadn't shown more than normal parental generosity, not even the two thin slices of our own that we sacrificed for him.

Jason also donates more blood to Canadian insects than anyone else I know. Ever since I was a kid, I have heard truly terrifying tales about northern fishing trips and bugs. My friend Jerry once told me that he nearly lost all semblance of self-control on a trip into the Quetico when hundreds of flies buzzed around his head and covered anything — rucksack, tackle box, or hat — that he set on the ground. They never bit him, but the incessant droning around his head was more than he could bear. He came out of the wilderness three days early.

Whenever I would see another friend, Arnie, after he had been to Canada, he would pull up his pant legs, roll down his socks, and show me dozens of black-fly bites on the pale whites of his ankles: "They crawl up your socks, the bloodthirsty little critters. And you never feel them at the time. But then later that day, usually when you're getting ready for bed, you notice pain around your ankles and you discover they're covered with these little purple bites. Do they ever sting!"

In general, though, in my family's trips to the U.P. and Canada, we have never been bothered too much by bugs. We are not usually bothered, that is, until the day has gone down to deep dusk. Then the mosquitoes materialize. Jon, Joel, Wanda, and I have decided that when it goes purple-gray in the west, it's time to get out of the boats and inside the cabin. Most people have had, at one time or another, mosquitoes buzz right into their mouth. But have you ever had a mosquito in your ear? Crawling up a nostril? Between the lens of your glasses and your eye?

Jason, on the other hand, has decided that when it's time to get out of the boats at night, it's time to begin fishing once more on the dock. So he stays out there, usually just off the edge of the glow of some security light, extremely active, casting with his right arm and waving his left to ward off mosquitoes. He's often quite successful attracting fish but never very successful warding off the mosquitoes. So when he finally comes in, his face, neck, and the back of his hands are covered with bites that look like strings of enormous pimples — but without the white center.

"Jay, you're a big mess of bites," Wanda says, with a mix of concern and scolding in her voice. "Why don't you forget fishing on the dock at night and stay inside with us?"

"Can't catch that big musky sitting on a couch in here."

"But you can't catch that big musky out there, either," Joel responds, mocking him.

"And," Jon says, "did you ever stop to think that when you're out there, the fish is not the real prey?"

"I repeat: 'You can't catch that big musky sitting on a couch in here.'"

And that's not the end of it. Jason will fish from docks no matter how foul the weather is. Not too long ago, for example, early in the last evening of our week at Eagle Lake, when we thought the wind might finally die down, it went up a pitch. Wind from the northwest, wind that flung swaths of rain and even June hail as it came, wind that earlier had whipped up whitecaps in our bay and that now blew foam off the tops of those waves as they curled. The boys and I, plus T-Gunz and Duzzer, were back from a four-wheel excursion to a nearby lake, a lake that everybody in camp called an "action" lake. But, though the wind was not as severe on that lake, much smaller and narrower than Eagle, the cold front that was driving the wind had apparently forced the fish deep and made them inactive — we had caught only a small walleye and a couple of skinny pike. We had had two or three musky follows, lazy follows, but nobody had had a hit.

Once we were back at the cabin on Eagle, Duzzer and I searched for a spot out of the wind and started the grill for the pork chops for supper, and the boys agreed to set the table and peel and boil the potatoes. Jason might have helped the others inside for a minute or two, but then he was back outside, still wearing several layers of clothes, including his new storm suit, his wool beanie, and his felt-pack boots. If he hadn't been carrying his medium-action spinning rod, I would have thought he was ready for ice fishing.

"What now? Where you going?" I asked. I couldn't believe he hadn't had enough that day. My face burned, my stomach was tight, and my head was still rocking.

"Down to the dock. Just for a few minutes before supper. I stashed my stuff inside, and I helped get the potatoes started.

Jon said he would finish those up. Joel and T-Gunz are just layin'
around — pooped — they're almost purple from windburn.
I'm gonna toss a jig and minnow from the dock."

"In wind like this? It's so wild out there you probably
should wear a life vest."

"What?"

"It's a joke, Jase. A joke."

"Dad, hasn't anyone ever told you you're not funny?"

"Nope. Anyway, just make sure you listen when we yell for
you. And don't let the wind or waves take you off the dock.
With all those clothes on, you'd be so heavy we'd have to winch
you out of the bay."

"Okay. Holler when supper's ready. See ya."

He started down the path to the dock, and I went inside to
pull off my boots and get out of my long underwear. I lay down
on my bunk for a couple of minutes, trying to get the inside of
my head to hold still.

"He can't! Joel's going to sit down and eat in a minute. He
can't come down there right now." It was Duzzer, outside my
window by the grill, shouting. "No, I'm telling you he can't
come down there right now. He's gonna eat. We're all gonna
eat. In a minute. We were just about to call you. What do you
need, anyway?"

Then I heard Joel hop off the couch in the sitting room and
scramble around tackle boxes to go out on the deck. I followed,
zipping my pants up as I went, but collided with Joel as he came
hustling back through the door.

"Jase needs help, and he needs it right now. Look out the
window. See his rod? No, over there — more to the left. He's
got a big fish on and he can't net it by himself. I've got to get

some boots on and get down there. There should be a big net in one of the boats."

His words put a charge in Jon and T-Gunz, and they got their own boots on and tore out of the cabin. I turned the potatoes down and followed them.

"I guess you're in charge of finishing supper up," I yelled at Duzzer as I ran out. "We'll be back. Hope it doesn't take all night. Maybe you'll be able to see some of the action from up here."

The dock at our camp had several sections. Running along the shoreline for about thirty yards was a base, supported by rusted iron supports at some points and by outcroppings of shield-rock at others. From this base three separate structures extended in parallel into the bay. The leftmost one, about twenty yards long, ran just this side of a bed of pencil reeds. The middle one was also about twenty yards long. And the one on the right ran out into the bay for about thirty-five yards and then turned ninety degrees and extended back to the left so that it shielded the water off the ends of both the middle and left structures. When I reached the base, I saw that Joel was holding an enormous net and standing next to Jason at the end of the middle structure. Jon and T-Gunz were a few yards back toward me, talking to two of the workers who had temporarily stopped gassing up the boats.

"What is it? Did you get a look?" I asked as I came up next to Jason and Joel, watching my footing on the wet planks.

"It's a musky," Jason said, giving a sharp little nod. "No sooner did I toss that jig and minnow out than I felt a clean take, and I set the hook hard. At first the fish was just swimming toward me, and I thought it was a walleye. I tried to walk back and grab a net out of that boat behind us, but then the fish turned and headed away toward that outer section of dock, smooth and easy and powerful, and I knew it was big. That's when I yelled to Duzzer to get Joel down here."

"That had to be eight or ten minutes ago. You've been fighting that fish all this time?"

"Yup. I'm taking my time, being really careful. I'm free-spooling quite a bit. Engage the reel and put as much pressure on her as I dare, gradually coaxing her in toward me, then free-spool when she turns and pulls away from me. There she goes again. See? I like watching the line cut the water. She's been trying to get over to that other section of dock, but so far I've been able to stop her each time. You'd think she'd get tired sooner or later."

"Unbelievable. That's not even your musky rod. How heavy is that line?"

"I'm in pretty good shape with the line — seventeen-pound mono. I should be using my musky rod, not this walleye rod, but my arms and shoulders got tired casting my musky gear on that other lake. I won't be able to put any serious pressure on this fish without shattering this rod, but I've got nothing else I have to do tonight, so I should be able to wear her down sooner or later."

"You're right," I said. "You'd better take your time. How you feeling? Got the strength to fight for a while?"

"I don't really feel tired. But I'm shaking all over — my knees are shaking, my hands are shaking. And I can feel my forearms about ready to cramp up."

Joel pulled me away from Jason and whispered: "Dad, you want to net it? I don't want to lose this fish for him."

"No, no — you take it. You can do it. Just don't let the size of that net make you think you can take it any way other than head on. Once Jase can lead it toward you and get its head up, go for it. Not before."

"All right, Jason," I said, turning back to him. "Do you think you can get that baby to head back this way? Gentle but steady. Will she turn? Can you move her at all?"

"I'm trying to . . . shoot, there she goes again. Off toward the outer dock." Jason was free-spooling again. "What does she want over there?"

"Chains!" a deep voice said. Joel, Jason, and I nearly launched ourselves into the water. Hubie, the resort owner and a well-known musky angler, had come up behind us and put his chin directly over Jason's shoulder.

"What, a little jumpy, are we? See, the end sections of this dock here are free floaters — nothing to worry about below. But that outer dock is chained to cement blocks on the bottom. You've got to keep her away from the chains. She wraps that line around them even once and the story's over. How long you been fighting her, anyways? You going to be able to land her sometime soon?"

"I've already spent about twenty minutes working her." Jason grimaced as the fish cruised along our section of the dock once more and then veered off back toward the chains. "And I'll spend whatever I need to. I'm not going to horse her. I never thought a fish could be so strong."

I glanced around. Jon and T-Gunz had moved off the dock into one of the moored boats and were leaning back lazily in padded chairs. The dockworkers were back to their work. And then Duzzer yelled down from our cabin: "Supper's going to get cold! Anybody planning to eat while it's still warm?"

I looked back to Jason. "How's she doing? Is she starting to let you lead her at all?"

"Yeah, some. Maybe you'd better get ready, Joel. I'll see if I can bring her in close."

"There she is — I see her! See that big green back?" It was Hubie again, now crouching between Jason and me. "Oh-oh!"

"Oh-oh what?" I felt little tremors in my chest muscles.

"He's not using a steel leader."

"No leader?" I asked. "Jase, you didn't tie on a steel leader?"

"Naw, I thought it would mess up the action of the jig and minnow."

Then I asked Hubie: "Did you see where she's got the jig?"

"Yeah, it's right in the corner of her mouth. That's as good of a place as there is. But if she rolls and gets the line on her gill cover, she slices right through it."

Jason heard him. "I'm hopin' she's too tired to thrash and roll much more. Joel, I'm going to try to lead her up close. That's it. That's it, you big girl. You know I'm going to get you, don't you?"

Jason started to emit little whine-grunts. "I think I can get her head up. Can you reach her, Joel? Close enough? I'll try a little more, a little more. Nice and easy. Here we go! Ouch, my hand just cramped up! Got to get that cramp out. There. Joel, get her, get her before she turns! Now, now, now . . . Joel. Not from the side! Head on! Head on! Not that way. I'll bring her in once more. Oops, there she goes again. Back toward those chains. I guess she's not as pooped as I thought. I'll have to turn her around again. Okay, here she comes. She's coming a little easier. I think this is it. Try it now!"

It was too much for me. I had to look away. I heard a tail

slap the surface hard and then a frenzy of splashing. I felt a dull ache in my back, low, just above my left hip. I was too scared to turn and look. But I knew I had to. And I saw Joel kneeling on the dock, both of his hands on the frame of the net, most of the net still in the water, and within its cords, thrashing as if it wasn't at all tired and had been surprised by the net, was the musky.

"Just keep her in the water; don't rough her up!" Hubie yelled. "Get the hook out and hold her up for some quick pictures. Then back in the water. They've got to be fifty-four inches to keep on Eagle, and I don't think she's more than that. A beauty, though, a real beauty. Probably about thirty pounds. All with a medium rod and no leader. And look — you've got a pretty good nick on your line a foot or so above the jig."

"I wouldn't keep her even if she was legal," Jason said. "And this line has always been pretty tough, even when it's nicked up. Dad, can you get a picture? Take a couple. And Jon, can you get a few pictures with the digital, too? Look at this fish! Will you look at this fish!"

After several pictures, Jason knelt and put the musky back in the water, held her upright, twisted her gently until some tone came back into her muscles, and eventually watched her swim away. After he stood back up, while the other boys were heading along the dock toward shore, their backs to us, I caught Jason's eye and then put one arm around him and gave him a side-to-side hug.

"Jase, Jase, Jase. Congratulations, man! Standing out here in the teeth of this storm, hooking that fish, fighting her so long and well, getting her to the net — it was all a thing of beauty!"

"I always knew I was gonna catch a fish like that from a

dock. I just didn't know which dock. Up till now, it's the fish of my life."

"Up till now," I said, "it's the fish of every one of our lives."

"And all it took was a little patience." ✆

PART THREE

Wives, Mothers, Trouble, Hope

Hope for a Full Recovery

"**O**kay, sir, I need you to tell me exactly what brings you here tonight." It was the emergency-room triage nurse, a model of earnest detachment. She had brought me a wheelchair and had started to question me as soon as I was seated. Wanda was still outside, parking the van.

"I don't know if I'm having a heart attack or what, but the pain and cramping are driving me wild. It started this morning with a cramp in the long muscle running down my side and back. Right here. It hurt, but I was still able to teach. Sorry, should have said that I'm a teacher. After class I decided that maybe something hot would help, so I went over to the gym and took a shower. Turned the water up as hard and hot as I could stand and moved around so that the stream ran up and down the left side of my back. It didn't help.

"So then what? I finally decided I wouldn't get anything done back in the office, so I went straight to the car and started for home. But just as I was coming around a building that was only about a hundred yards from the gym, a flash like an electric shock shot up both sides of the back of my neck, swept over the top of my ears and across my forehead, and made my eyes tear up. I pulled over and was about to signal someone for help, but then I thought, *Gut it out — you can make it home. Just don't plow into anybody.* I made it home squinting first through one eye, then the other. But even after I lay down, I was miserable. Left side, right side, on my back, on my stomach, I didn't know what to do with myself. I was cramping all over — first my side and then my lower back, then my hamstrings, then a calf muscle, then a foot, then back up high, across my chest. I couldn't find any position to be comfortable in, and I still can't. My muscles have gone wild."

"You have pain in your chest?"

"Yeah, right across the bottom of my pecs."

"On a scale from one to ten, with ten being the worst, how bad would you say the pain is?"

"That's tough. I guess I would say, since this is as close to frantic as I've ever been — and I almost cut four fingers off on a table saw once — close to an eight."

"The doctor will order some morphine."

"No morphine. Morphine makes me vomit. Makes everybody in my family vomit."

"Okay, I'll make a note. We're going to move you into Exam Room 2. The doctor will be in to see you momentarily." Wanda came through the doors from the parking lot, scanned the room anxiously before she spotted me, and came over to walk alongside the chair as an orderly wheeled me toward the exam rooms.

When Dr. Stemat came in, he asked, "Well, Mr. Vande Kopple, so what brings you here tonight?"

I have to tell the whole story again? I wondered, initially feeling more irritation than pain. But it was clear that he wanted to hear the details from me, not the nurse, and he listened attentively as I described my day.

"Okay, I'll give you something now for the pain, and then an orderly will take you down the hall for a CAT scan of your chest."

"Better not use morphine. Morphine makes me vomit."

"Really? We'll try something else then. Here's your nurse." He turned and whispered something to her. And then louder: "Yes, go ahead and start him on it right away. Mr. Vande Kopple, you'll start to feel it in just a couple of minutes. The orderly will be here soon."

When Wanda had had a CAT scan about a year earlier, I had decided that I could never get inside even one of the fairly thin tubes without worrying that the walls would gradually expand and ultimately crush me. But by the time the technicians had me flat on the platform and lined up properly, I was just loopy enough not to care what anyone did to me.

"Okay, that's it — back to the emergency room. As soon as we have these pictures developed, we'll bring them over."

Back in Exam Room 2, I felt myself starting to drift. *You absolutely have to hear everything the doc says*, I chided myself. I tried to count the dots in a stained corner of a ceiling tile. Then I had to start again. Then once more.

"Don't fight it — just let yourself sleep," Wanda said. "It might take them some time to bring the pictures. I'll make notes about everything they say. Meanwhile, I'm going to call Jon and tell him where we are. Hope the boys went ahead with some supper on their own."

A technician's voice brought me back. *Where's the doctor?* I wondered. *Why's he saying all this to me?*

"Nothing obviously wrong with your heart, at least from these angles. But you've got a growth on your left adrenal. And see these spots on your liver? The report says 'mets to liver.' See that — 'mets'? It's short for 'metastasized.' Do you know what that means?"

Then Dr. Stemat's voice cut in: "Let me see that. And I'll need a word with you in the hallway when I'm finished here. Okay, Mr. Vande Kopple, try to ignore what you've just heard. Let's see. It probably won't surprise you to learn that you're not going home tonight. We'll have to run some tests on that growth, but right now we're going to try to find out what's happening with your heart. I've called a cardiologist, and I've arranged for a room up in cardiac intensive care. You'll be in good hands."

As they wheeled my bed out of the exam room, I rolled slightly on my side and saw Wanda in the corner near the window, her face in her hands.

That was my life? I mused as I dozed off.

"Talk about rotten luck." It was Duzzer, four and a half months later, on the deck of our cabin overlooking Myers Bay on Ontario's Eagle Lake: "Here we cram six people and all their equipment in a van and drive thirteen hours one day and five hours the next, and as we get closer and closer, all of us are going bonkers we're so excited to get out on the water. But then we get here, and we step out of the van into a freezing northwest wind and find whitecaps on the bay. We're pretty sheltered here, but still, those waves are huge. Just think what it must be like outside the bay. Maybe we should just stay in the cabin tonight and play some Rook."

"What? That doesn't sound like you at all," I said. "I've never once seen you stay back when you had a chance to get out on the water."

"True, but those waves are bigger than anything you and I have ever dared fish in before, even at Drummond Island."

"You can stay here if you want. And the boys can stay. They'll probably want to get at the pool table in the main lodge. But I can't stay back. I've got to get out there."

"Give me a break! You've got to fish every possible second? That's a gale out there."

"We're prepared," I said. "We can put five or six layers on, add our rain suits and heavy boots, and fish in the lee of one of those islands out there off the mouth of the bay. I know you're supposed to fish for muskies on windblown points, but in weather like this we wouldn't be able to control the boat very well. The odds might not be great, so you don't have to go if you don't want to, but I'm going to get bundled up and give it a shot."

"All right. Okay, I guess I'll go. But if the waves are so bad that we start turning kidneys into pinballs, we're coming back in. Deal?"

"That's fair. Let's move it."

A half hour later we sat in the lee of Colonel's Island, each of us taking quiet inventory of the damage the wave-slamming might have done to us. I had my hand inside my parka and was running my fingertips lightly over where my abdomen had been stapled shut after my operation.

"That was the roughest ride I can remember," I said, forcing a laugh.

"Real funny. It's not as rough for you, back there by the engine. I think my tailbone is cracked. And I feel like I've got to pee already, and I made sure I went just before we left the cabin.

How am I going to find my way through about fifty layers? Zippers don't always line up, you know."

"Just wait a minute or two — it'll pass."

"It'll pass. It'll pass. Easy for you to say — you don't have to live with my bladder," Duzzer said. "Anyway, what're you gonna use?"

"I think I'll try my new Bull Dawg. Supposed to be good up here."

"Hope you did your pushups before you left. That thing must weigh about ten pounds. You're welcome to it. I'm going to try out this silver Bomber Magnum. It comes through the water really easily. And I can cast it a mile."

I slowly backtrolled us as we worked our way from east to west, casting around the ledges that extended out from the shoreline of Colonel's Island. Then, before we got into the frenzy of whitecaps out past the western point of the island, I turned and worked us back from west to east. No hits. Not even a momentary snag in the weeds.

Duzzer was looking around, scanning the water. "What's that out there?" he asked. "Deeper. It's got that rusty color of the kind of reefs we've always found fish by."

I backtrolled away from the island, still in its lee, but out toward deeper water. His eyes hadn't failed him. He had spotted a crescent-shaped reef, probably forty to fifty yards if you measured from one of its tips across the mouth of the crescent to the other; its highest point was two to three feet below the surface. In the water inside the crescent was a bed of thick cabbage weeds.

"This is perfect," I said, making sure we didn't drift into the weeds. "Let's start at this end of the weedbed and work our way along. There's got to be a big girl hiding out in a place like this. It's better than most of the sketches in magazines."

As we started to cast, we went quiet. Tense. Imagining a hit with every turn of our reels. All the way along the outside edge of the weeds. Then back. Then we moved in closer and ground our biggest spinnerbaits right through the weeds. Again two passes. Then we burned Top Raiders on the surface above the weeds. A pass to the west. Then one to the east.

"This is unbelievable," Duzzer was surveying the extent of the weedbed. "I've never seen such a good-looking spot. Can't believe we didn't get a hit. Not even a follow. Maybe we should head in. Not smart to get caught out here after dark."

"It's about time. But let's make one more pass, with different surface lures. It's not full dark yet." And then I turned away from Duzzer, glanced toward the diffused glow of the lights marking the dock of our camp, and inhaled deeply. *Every cast,* I said to myself, *is a cast into the future.*

The morning after I was admitted to cardiac intensive care, I met the specialists.

The first one in was Dr. Lee, an oncologist. He had taken a close look at my pictures, he said, and in his view the spots on my liver were probably not life-threatening: "CAT scans can be calibrated so finely these days that they can almost pick up individual molecules. What you've got on your liver looks like a few small cysts — we'll do some blood tests to check liver functions — but I know lots of people who have spots on their liver like that."

"What about that growth on my adrenal?"

"We'll have to wait and see. I've told the nurse that I want total urine collection for the next twenty-four hours. Here's the container. That growth could be something harmless — an incidentaloma, we call them — or it could be causing the adrenal to secrete. That's what the urine test will show. Right now I would say that it doesn't look malignant. It's regular in shape, it's not massive, and it has a clear margin all the way around it. So my judgment now is that our first priority is to make sure your heart is okay. I'm going to tell the cardiology team to proceed. We won't get the results of the urine test back for a few days, but if that test is negative, then you can just make an appointment to see me in about thirty days to discuss what, if anything, to do about that growth. Hope things go well for you."

Check that one off, then, I said to myself. If he doesn't need to see me for thirty days, that growth can't be too serious.

Although I have never had any fully formed imaginary friends, I do occasionally have more than one voice seeking attention within me, and one of them became insistent just then: Sure, it might not be too serious. Maybe you can wait thirty days. But what if the doctor said that because there's no hope? Maybe there's nothing he can do for you. Anything you absolutely have to take care of in the next month?

Dr. Infada, the cardiologist, swept into the room at that moment and drew my attention away from the other voice. He was brusque, confident, in a hurry.

"The enzyme tests they ran on your blood last night came back inconclusive. So we don't know if there's any heart damage. But you're in luck," he said, grinning. "We wanted to get you in for some catheterization and couldn't find an opening at first, but someone cancelled for this afternoon, so you're on for two o'clock."

"Is this a serious procedure?" I asked. "I've heard of it but don't know many details."

"It should be routine. I've got three or four of these scheduled for this afternoon. Clockwork."

"Is it something I have to be put under for? I'm not in love with losing consciousness."

"Not completely. We'll probably sedate you lightly. You won't feel much at all — a little pinch in the groin. And then you'll be able to watch the monitors and see parts of your heart working. It's fascinating. If you need any stents, we can insert them with the catheter. See you this afternoon. Someone will come to get you a half hour before the procedure."

The "someone" turned out to be two female orderlies, both young, energetic, full of wisecracks and jokes. As they helped me out of bed, the one taking my left arm asked: "Still got your drawers on?"

I laughed, remembering the many dictates, none highly nuanced, that had been repeated in our workplace sexual-harassment training.

"Absolutely. Why?" I asked.

"Drop 'em," she said.

"Huh?"

"The doctors are going to start the catheter through a point in your groin, and the nurse will have to give you a little shave before that."

"This shoal must extend from the island toward the mainland for two or three hundred yards, and I can see good-looking weeds all along the edges." It was early, but Joel was casting his in-line spinner as if he had stored up energy all night just for this.

He and I had gotten up before all the others the morning after the windstorm and had decided to head out together for a while before breakfast. On leaving the bay where our camp was situated, we had skirted Colonel's Island on our way farther south, and had soon found a large shoal east of Boathouse Island. We had started near the island and were fishing our way along the shoal toward the mainland.

"I'm having a little trouble taking even this fairly small section of the lake in," I said as I reeled, "all this water and structure."

"It's my first time out, but I can see what you mean. It looks like things just go on and on: rocky points and islands and bays and weedbeds all over the place." Then suddenly, with a barely audible hiss, Joel was bending over the gunnel, thrusting the tip of his rod into the water, vigorously outlining a large subsurface figure eight.

"What?" My eyes weren't as sharp as his.

"Unbelievable! My breath's gone! I should have been . . . I should have been more ready. I might have had it. My L-turn was a bit late. I should have started a second or two earlier. What a musky! It was the biggest fish I've ever seen. Like a bronze torpedo. A huge mouth! That thing could swallow a schnauzer. It came up out of that dark slot between those two ledges. Not super fast. Not really an attack. More like a little look-things-over. When it got close I froze for a fraction of a second, and it turned. I should have started my circle earlier. Whew! You got your hook file? I've got to touch up my hooks. If she comes up again, maybe she'll nip, and then I'm going to get a hook into her."

"That wasn't even twenty casts for you, was it? Not even fifteen? What a start! If things keep up like that, I'm guessing that everyone in our group will say we should never even consider any other fishing camp."

"You're probably right," Joel said. "There's only one problem."

"What's that?"

"You don't know? You have absolutely no clue?"

"Not a clue."

"It's the cabin. To get to the bathroom, everyone has to walk through the common sitting area."

"So?"

"Well, in a cabin like that, we should probably make it a rule that Duzzer and you, you old guys, shouldn't be walking around in your underwear."

"Where does this come from?" I said, feeling the raspy edge of annoyance.

"After the two of you came in from fishing in that storm last night and started parading back and forth from your room to the bathroom, Jon, Jason, T-Gunz, and I had a chance to talk, and we decided that we've got to lay down the law. You walk around with your flabby bellies showing, and you wear those whitey-tighties that are practically worn out in the back. Those are gross. We think you should stay fully dressed while you walk around the cabin. Either that or maybe check with the ladies who clean the cabins to see if they have robes you can wear. If they don't and you absolutely have to walk around like that, maybe you should get a room in that little hotel in Vermillion Bay — it's only about a mile and a half from camp."

"You know what I think?" I said. "I think you guys are a bunch of prudes. Just because you wear those boxers with all the patterns and pictures on them doesn't mean that we have to give up our plain white briefs. We go along and start wearing boxers, and then you guys will say we have to start sagging. No thanks. I don't really see what the big deal is. This week it's just a bunch of guys staying in a fishing cabin together. I didn't happen to see any of your girlfriends around. Duzzer and I can't walk around the cabin in our underwear? You can't be serious. All we do is make a quick little run from our bedroom to the shower. If we have a touch of old man's disease in the morning, you guys aren't awake enough to be bothered. Probably what's behind all this is that you guys aren't really comfortable with your bodies. Maybe we should make a rule that once we're back at the cabin at the end of the day, all of us should walk around in our underwear. What do you think about that? Huh, big guy? Maybe it'd be good for you to walk around in your boxers."

"You'd need more money than you've got for that," Joel said.

"Money? For what?"

"If I walked around in my boxers, it'd be like a famous commercial."

"You got to be kidding. A commercial? A commercial for what?"

And then Joel, twenty-one years old, almost certainly as big and strong and virile as he's ever going to be in this life, looked at me with calm bravado and snorted, "A commercial for a body that's dead sexy, old man!"

"A feo what? How do you spell that?" I didn't recognize what Dr. Lighter, my primary-care physician, had called the growth on my adrenal. A week after the cardiologists had determined that I hadn't had a heart attack and could go home, his office called and said that he needed to see me as soon as possible. I had skipped lunch to keep the appointment.

"It's p-h-e-o-c-h-r-o-m-o-c-y-t-o-m-a. It's a dusky-colored tumor, usually on one or the other adrenal gland. They're called the ten-percent tumors, since only about ten percent of them are malignant. But even if they're not cancerous, they cause the adrenal to secrete. And any more adrenaline in the system than normal is dangerous. When we do a urine-measurement test on a person without a pheo, we usually find about twenty-five milliliters of adrenaline. Your urine had 430 milliliters. So I think that this tumor caused your emergency-room episode. You had a cortisol crisis or an adrenal storm. Somehow you must have put pressure on a spot near your adrenal or had a blow to the back. I can well imagine that you thought the top of your head was going to blow off."

"Unbelievable!" I said. "I might have caused the whole thing myself. I took a shower and turned up the water as hard and hot as I could and aimed it right on my lower back. On the left."

"I see. And since the water was hot, you probably also drew all kinds of blood to the area. That would stimulate the gland as well."

"I can't believe I brought this all on by myself. But something bad was bound to happen sooner or later, right?"

"Right."

"So now what?"

"It has to come out," Dr. Lighter said.

"I have to have surgery? I was hoping I wouldn't have to be cut."

"No choice. If you leave a pheo in, no matter how much we medicate you, you'll probably start having worse headaches than any you've ever had before, and even if you think you can live with the headaches, sooner or later the pheo will lead to a stroke or a heart attack. A big shot of adrenaline and your blood pressure will go off the scale."

"Do you have a surgeon to recommend?" I asked. "I know one, but I don't think he does this kind of stuff. Oh, another thing — the wife of one of my colleagues had her gallbladder taken out, and they did it with a tiny slit and a scope. She was back to work in about three days. Any chance my procedure can be done the same way?"

"When the pheo is on the right side, surgeons often can work with a scope. But yours is on the left, and the left adrenal is packed in among so many other organs that I'm afraid you'll have to have an open adrenalectomy."

"Where are they going to cut me?"

"I've had only one other patient who had a pheo — these tumors are really rare. So I can't be sure. The best I can do is to predict on the basis of his scar. From your perspective looking down, the incision will probably start a couple inches to the right and about three inches above your navel. It will slant up to a point above your navel and then angle down gently about eight inches toward your left hipbone. When you first check it out after surgery, you'll probably be shocked — you'll see a row of metal staples at that point, but once the staples come out, such incisions usually heal up well. I'll have my nurse set up a time for a consult with the surgeon I have in mind. He operated on my wife just last fall."

When I got back to the office, Barb, our departmental secretary, knocked on my office door and wanted to hear the details. I had told her what my doctor visit was about.

"You know, I've had more operations than I can count," Barb said. "I've been cut from stem to stern, and then cut again — I've got scars on my scars. So you can talk to me. Are you worried?"

"When I was lying in the hospital after my so-called heart trouble," I replied, "I suspected that sooner or later I'd have to have some kind of operation, and I thought I'd just tough it out one more time — even in those few days in the hospital, I got used to going through a bunch of procedures. But now that I know for certain that I'll have to have an adrenal gland out, I'm pretty jittery. And I don't think it's just all the adrenaline that's usually in me."

"What's it all about? Worried about the aftereffects of the anesthesia?"

"Not too much. I know some of the people around the office say that it took them two to three months after anesthesia to feel that they had their head on right again, but I guess I'm not too bent out of shape by that. Who knows about my head, anyway?"

"How about the helplessness or the embarrassment? The invasion? If they have to get all the way back to your adrenal, they're going to have to lay you wide open and then start moving things around. And you'll have to have a catheter."

"A catheter? I already had that. They checked my heart and found that it was in pretty good shape. Had to be in good shape or that adrenaline rush would have blown something."

"No, not that. You'll need a catheter for urine."

"No way! Where would it go?"

"You know where it'll go."

"You gotta be kidding me!"

"Nope," she said, shaking her head slowly.

"Well, I wasn't even aware of that, so I couldn't really be worried about that then, could I?"

"Probably not. But what about all the pain afterwards? Cut through all that abdominal muscle, and you're going to hurt for a long time. Just hope you don't have to sneeze until weeks after surgery. And make sure you don't watch any funny movies for a while after you get home. I watched *Grumpy Old Men* a day after I came home from my last surgery, and I thought I was going to tear open."

"You know, it's not really that either. But just talking about all this has made it clearer. I think I know what I'm most jittery about."

"What?"

"It's the going to sleep," I said, "the letting go."

As our week at Eagle Lake went on, we gradually extended the range of our excursions away from the lodge. On Tuesday, the six of us, in our small armada, agreed that we must have found Bottleneck Point. Then we motored farther south, around the eastern shore of an island, and at last sat bobbing just off the north coast of Portage Bay in the late afternoon.

"Want to try some of the coves along the shore here in Portage Bay?" I shouted to the others. "If I remember right, Hubie had lots of spots in Portage Bay marked on his big map in the lodge."

"You sure this is Portage Bay?" Jason yelled back.

"Yup. I paid close attention to the map on the way down."

"Okay, let's give it a try."

"Right. Let's hit that cove over there first. Split up, cover as much water as possible, and meet way in the back."

Joel, Duzzer, and I were sharing a boat that day. As we moved into progressively shallow water, we noticed widely spaced clusters of pencil reeds.

"Looks like prime spinnerbait territory to me," Duzzer whispered. "Bounce 'em off the reeds, snap 'em around a little bit, and hello fishie!"

On his first cast a pike hit and tried to wrap his line around the base of a reed.

"Don't you mess with me," he cackled and eventually pulled the fish off the reed and loosened his drag as the near-thirty-incher dove, went under the boat, and then turned and tried to take the line around the propeller. Just then Joel had his own hit.

"Another pike?" I had turned to watch.

"Not sure. No, not a pike. It's a big walleye. Look at the gold. And the shoulders on it. It's a double, the first double of the day!"

"Yeah, so who's gonna net my fish?" Duzzer was trying to sound serious.

"I would," I said, chuckling, "but I just nailed one, too. Feels pretty good. Hey, look at us — it's a triple! And nobody with a free hand to take a picture. The net's by Joel's feet, Duz — you'll have to land your own fish."

That was the first of several triples, made all the more likely since when one of us got a hit, he would take more than the usual time fighting his fish, waiting for the two others to hook up. There was some mist in the air, and later a steady and chilling rain, but we hardly noticed, except on the backs of our hands. We hadn't seen any muskies in the bay, but each of was well up into the teens in numbers of pike and walleyes landed. And it looked like the other boat was doing just as well. All of us were most intent on coming home with a picture of a big musky or two, maybe fifty inches plus, but none of us wanted to break away very quickly from the numbers game we had gotten into.

When we were finally back at the dock, around six o'clock, Joel and T-Gunz asked if I would drive them into town to Bobbi's Baits so they could buy a couple of the Inhaler spinners they had noticed in storage compartments in the guides' boats. They wanted to give them a try after supper. The van was a rental, and Duzzer and I were the only legal drivers of record.

"I will if someone agrees to start supper. Jon, you will? Okay then, let's go. Get out of this rain, and wait in the van. Just let me run in and peel off a layer or two."

But when I joined them in the van and turned the key, I heard nothing. No faltering turn of the engine. No clicking. Nothing.

I must be doing something wrong, I thought. I took out the key, checked it, and watched myself as I methodically inserted and turned it.

"Oh, brother," I said, "we've got a dead battery. Maybe worse. Usually you get at least some clicks. I didn't hear a thing." The three of us got back out, and I opened the hood, not sure what I should be looking for.

"What's up? Checking the oil?" Duzzer had noticed the open hood from the kitchen window of the cabin and had come out on the side deck.

"No," I said, suddenly feeling my pulse in my neck. "I tried to start it twice and got nothing. No trip to Bobbi's tonight, I guess. Here we are a thousand miles from home with a van that won't start. What were we planning for tomorrow? Exploring the western arm? Well, probably the five of you should head over there and check it out. I've got to get this taken care of. It might be best for me to ask about a wrecker and get this beast towed to Dryden. That's probably the nearest town with anything like a decent repair shop. Maybe I should take the day, get the van checked out, and try to get it fixed. It might be just the battery, but it could be a lot more, and we've got all those miles to get back around the top of Superior — "

"Bill," Duzzer cut in, "I don't know if you noticed on the way up, but those dome lights in back are really touchy. Bump them a little to one side or the other and they come on and stay on. Somebody must have gotten into the back this morning or maybe last night and bumped a dome light without noticing. That's all it is, I bet — a dome light drained the battery."

"I'd love to believe it. All we'd need is a jump. But on the way up here we had the 'Service Engine Soon' light flickering as we finished those hard climbs, so I'm not feeling too confident about this van. If I have to miss a day of fishing, then that's what I'll have to do. If I could find out exactly what's wrong with this van, I wouldn't have at least half my mind buzzing about it when we're out on the lake."

Duzzer wouldn't give up: "You can't miss a whole day of fishing, especially in the west arm, water you've been talking about all week, just because a dumb dome light drained the battery. I've got an idea: tomorrow morning we'll write a little note saying we have a dead battery, and we'll put it up on the desk in the main lodge with a key to the van and ask anyone who reads it for a charge or a jump. When we get back from the west arm tomorrow night, I bet the van will start. They work with so many boat batteries here that they're bound to have chargers and stuff."

"You'd trust that? How do you know that anyone's going to see that note? And if they do, they'll probably think it's a prank. And then we'll be one day closer to when we have to get back on the road, one day closer with a van that won't start."

"I got the idea from an old *In-Fisherman*. Doug Stange was writing about one of his early trips to Canada, when the gravel road they were on damaged some part of his truck. I don't remember exactly what part — maybe something with the suspension had to be welded. Anyway, he parked the truck between the road and a river, left a note on the window asking someone to fix the damaged part, and then he and a friend took off in a canoe down the river fishing. When they got back three days later, lo and behold, someone had fixed their truck."

"Very nice story. The only trouble is, that's not the world I live in. Leave a note, take off and have a good time fishing, and come back to find that all your problems have been solved? Some part of me would love to believe that, but. . . ."

"You know something," Duzzer said, "you worry too much."

"You know something: maybe you should worry a little more. I hear that worry is mainly a matter of imagination, and that's something it might be good for you to have more of."

"I've got plenty of imagination. Whoever said I needed more imagination?"

"Just look at what's happening here. I can imagine all kinds of things that could be wrong with the van, and I can imagine about a thousand ways this could mess up the rest of our trip. And all you can come up with is an idea to leave a little note and the key in the main lodge."

"If having more imagination means I could come up with more stuff as scary as what you think up, then I'll pass on it. I'll pass for sure. Just try the note. If nobody does anything, we'll still have a couple of days left for van repairs, and then I'll go along and help. But let's all fish the west arm together tomorrow."

"All right. But if we get back tomorrow and this thing still doesn't start, then we're taking it in for sure."

"That's what I said," Duzzer said, raising his tone. "I told you I'd go along and help. Maybe you weren't paying attention — what with your imagination working so hard. If you leave a note and the key, we won't have to be taking the van anywhere."

The west arm was even more beautiful than I had imagined. From a distance it looked as if the hills along the coast, all a slightly frosted green, lay like an enormous cloak with tight folds at irregular intervals. When we got into the arm itself, we found that some of these folds opened only into tiny inlets but that others wound through the hills before leading to bays a mile or more in circumference. The whole arm seemed to invite us to motor farther and farther to the west and then, occasionally, to veer off and explore one or another finger bay. Many sections of the west arm had deeper water than the rest of Eagle Lake, and these sections were so clear that they led all of us to peer over the side, point, and start mostly playful debates about the best words for colors and structures. In one cranny between two charcoal-colored boulders I saw what I think was the biggest smallmouth of my life. But when I dropped a brownish tube near it, the giant vanished into the shadows.

To some extent, I loved our little expedition; I would have loved it with my whole mind had I been able to forget about our van. But I managed not to think about the van all the time, and I was able to show something like genuine excitement when Jason hooked and landed a thirty-pound lake trout while casting for muskies.

As we raced across Vermillion Bay on our way back to the camp, I felt a sense of relief. *At least now we'll see,* I thought. *Duzzer is going to be having some words for supper tonight.*

As we approached the dock, I looked up to the little bluff on which our cabin sat and noticed that the van was exactly where it had been in the morning. And when I made it up the pathway from the dock, I walked to the front end of the van to see if anyone had left some greasy fingerprints or smudges, the telltale signs of what would have been altruistic activity. No smudges. Just the solidified internal juices — mostly green and yellow — of insects that had flown into our path on our way north.

"You might want to come and look at this," Duzzer called from the open back door of the cabin.

"What? What now?"

"Just come and look. Check out what's on the table."

I took my time up the stairs and past my grinning fishing buddy, who started whistling Michigan State's fight song as I passed him. And then I saw what he was referring to: someone had cleared a little space amid the pamphlets and maps we had left on the table, and in that space I saw the key to our van. Next to the key was a scrap of paper on which — I had to move closer so that I could read it — were three short words: "Saw your note."

The anesthesiologist, I thought, looked competent. He had introduced himself shortly after the nurse in pre-op had used soap and surgical thread to pull my wedding ring off.

"The real challenge in this procedure is a possible blood-pressure crisis. When the surgeon clamps off the blood vessel running from the adrenal, he will step back, and we will all focus on what your blood pressure does. You have to know that Dr. Rodriguez is one of the best surgeons I have ever worked with. And I see from your records that Dr. Lighter has prepped you well. You've been on an alpha-blocker for how long?"

"Almost two weeks — that's the most expensive drug I've ever heard of."

"And you've been drinking lots of Gatorade to get your electrolytes up. Also eating lots of salty snacks, right?"

"Right. I think I've had more chips in the past two weeks than in the year prior to that."

"That's good. We need your blood volume up. As I said, you've been prepped really well. You've probably read about people dying on the table because of a pheo, but that happens mainly when the surgery is for something else and they discover a pheo by accident. But as I said, we know what we're going in for. I'll insert a wire in one of the big vessels in your throat, and I'll run that wire right into your heart so that I can monitor your blood pressure at every single heartbeat. I have medication if it spikes. And I have another medication if it bottoms out. Any questions? No? Just remember — you're going to be fine. Really, you'll be fine. That being said, I'm going to give you a little something right now to take the edge off."

And then an orderly came, Wanda pressed her lips to mine, and I went through the gleaming doors. I was somewhat proud that, despite the "little something," I was noticing so many details. As we rolled down the hallway, I thought of all the sermons I had heard about death as the ultimate certainty for all humankind. What I needed was some language that would prepare me to see the face of God, maybe in the next twenty or thirty minutes, a sermon about "my only comfort in life and death," with the emphasis on the "my." As I came into the operating room, still noticing details, I saw more people than I had expected, at least eight, all masked and looking at me intently.

Why so many people? I asked myself. It was then that I started praying as hard as I ever have, asking God for forgiveness until my very last moment of consciousness. I was trying to do all that I could to ensure that no sinful thought could worm itself into that last fleeting moment between final petition and ultimate injection.

When I opened my eyes, I made out three figures off to my right, dimly backlit. *Who? Who can it be?* I wondered. And then the one in the middle moved toward me slowly, almost as if floating. The other two followed, at a slight distance. I couldn't make out their faces. *Where are my glasses?* I wondered. *I need to see who they are.*

"You're awake, just about right on schedule." It was Wanda, some questioning mixed with relief in her voice. My dad and mom came up on either side of her.

"What time is it?" I asked. "How long have I been out?" All I could remember was someone tightening a strap across my ankles in the operating room. I had heard things about surgeons using gravity to move organs around.

"Surgery took about two and a half hours, and you've been in surgical intensive care for another hour or so." Wanda leaned over and let her lips linger on my forehead.

"Am I going to be okay? Did they talk to you after surgery?"

"Both the surgeon and the anesthesiologist spent some time with us," my dad said. "They said they were really pleased with how everything went. I guess you were as well prepared for this operation as anyone they've ever seen. They had to do a little rearranging to get to where they could see the growth. But they got it, and they said it didn't look dangerous. They had to send it to the lab, of course, but on the surface it didn't look cancerous. And through the whole thing, you hardly bled. If I remember everything they said, they didn't even have to give you any blood. Do you remember much?"

"As I watched them strapping my ankles down, I was praying so hard that I was running words together in my head. And then I was gone."

Thursday was the day for our fly-out. We were told to be out on the dock at six a.m., when a floatplane from Wilderness Air would pick us up and fly us about sixty miles north to Oak Lake, a relatively shallow, dark-bottomed lake through which the Zizania River flowed. This was to give us all a taste of Canadian wilderness and put us on some walleyes. "Lately," the word around camp was, "everyone flying to Oak has been slaughtering the walleyes, big walleyes."

Before we boarded the plane, the dock boy gave us three bait buckets, each holding a gross of gasping minnows, and Hubie, the lodge owner, gave us a Xerox copy of a rough map of Oak Lake with spots highlighted in red on it. All the points as well as the shorelines of most islands, I noticed.

I had told everyone to eat plenty of toast so that their stomachs wouldn't be knocking around once we were in the air, and they had taken my advice, but the flight turned out to be smoother than a train ride. We landed on a southern bay of Oak, filled the gas tanks in the boats hauled up on the shore, and then Duzzer and I followed the boys' two boats as they headed around a point in our bay and stopped in the first little inlet they came to.

"This isn't even highlighted on the map," I yelled over to them.

"Big deal," Joel shouted back, "it looks good. We might as well try it. We flew up here to fish, not ride around."

"All right. We'll all try it. But I think that sooner or later we should head down to that island in the narrows."

We bobbed in the mouth of the bay while we all tied on quarter-ounce jigs and hooked a minnow through the lips. Then we split up so as to make three different drifts across the inlet. I thought we would catch nothing.

But as we drifted, Jon and Jason each caught a small pike, and T-Gunz hooked a twelve-inch walleye. As we all came up to the shore, Joel called over:

"Nothing, huh? That's three fish on one drift. I wouldn't exactly call that nothing."

"Get real!" I said impatiently. "Everyone says that on Oak you slaughter fish, even when it's as windy as it is today, and a couple of skinny pike and an adolescent walleye is not exactly a slaughter. Catching that walleye is almost child abuse! Let's head down to the narrows."

I heard some mumbling from the other boats, a couple of spikes of laughter, but then they waved at me to take the lead. It wasn't hard to find the narrows: the river got skinny as it made a sharp turn to the right, and just off the right-hand point lay a teardrop of an island.

"Let's start up by the shore of the island," I said, "and let the wind take us drifting into deeper water."

So much of what I had heard throughout my life about walleye fishing turned out not to be true of the fishery at Oak Lake. I thought you needed to jig with your line perfectly vertical in the water, but we were able to hook up even when the wind gusted and had us drifting away from the island with our lines out behind us at forty-five degrees. I thought you needed to use the lightest possible leader, so Duzzer and I both tied on a section of six-pound fluorocarbon line, practically invisible under water. But Jon and Jason later told me that they had fished the entire day with seventeen-pound mono, and they ended up catching more and bigger fish than Duzzer and I did. I thought that the more lively the minnow, the more likely you were to attract walleye, but all the boys proved this wrong: they fished with dead minnows, even minnow heads and tails, and they did well.

Those walleyes seemed hungry, even desperate. Our portable depth finders showed that the water just off the shore of the island was about eight feet deep, and we hardly ever caught anything as we started our drifts, but once we got out into fifteen feet of water, we got busy. Once we were blown into thirty-five feet of water, it seemed that we had drifted past the school, though occasionally one boat would drift farther than normal and then catch the biggest walleye to that point in the day. If we ever made a drift and didn't get a hit, we were startled. *How can this be?* we would ask ourselves.

That day on the water, as so many similar days, turned into a contest. Who led in numbers? (Jon ended up winning with thirty-six.) Who had the biggest fish? (I led for a while with a twenty-five-incher, but again Jon ended up winning, with a twenty-eight.) Who caught the most fish with a single minnow? (Jason caught five walleyes with one minnow, which by the end was only a shred of flesh attached to a tail.)

If people had been fishing near us that day, they would have heard an astonishing amount of noise (another rule of walleye fishing that we broke, with no ill effects on our fishing): bragging, taunting, counting, whooping, laughing, even some singing. It didn't even seem right to stop for ten minutes and unwrap the jelly sandwiches we had packed so early in the morning.

I sometimes tell people (I really have to trust them to tell them) that as a child I had a crippling fear of the whole notion of eternity. I would sit in church and hear the choir singing about a longing for life without end in heaven, and I would wonder, *How can anyone want that?* And I often could not get to sleep at night because I would start thinking of what it must be like to live ten thousand years and then look ahead and see no possible end, no closing off of the arc of actions, not even some little breaks from all our heavy consciousness.

I still have this fear, though now I've learned that I have to try to block it. When I first feel one of its sharp fingernails, I force myself to think about something else. I can't even toy with it, as I can with some of my fears. Considering it even a little means inviting all of its paralyzing effects in — the sweat along my hairline, the thrumming heart, the lightheaded isolation, the panic of being trapped by something unknowable.

But when I was catching all those walleyes on Oak Lake, counting and bragging while I rebaited and got my line back in the water as fast as I could, all sense of time fell away and I was fishing in the wonder of a continuous now. *That was a beauty, I would think. Now I've got to get another.* So when Duzzer said that it was 4:30 and that we should pack up and head back to make sure we would meet the plane on time, I was a little surprised to find myself thinking that I wanted the fishing to go on and on, walleye after walleye after walleye.

"One more drift," I said, resisting his edict. "We've got time for one more drift."

"Okay, but just one. I don't think it's a good idea to have the pilot land and have to wonder where we are."

I motored from the deep water back to the island, hooked up a fresh minnow, released my line, and started jigging. Nothing. Nothing. Maybe. No, still nothing. Wait a second. There it was again. Just a tap, the subtlest of taps. I dropped my rod tip slowly toward the water, giving some extra line, what Hubie called "bowing to the fish." Then I braced myself, whipped my rod skyward, and felt the resolute presence.

When I was moved from surgical intensive care to a regular room, I thought I would finally be able to rest. *Maybe here, I*

thought, *I'll be able to sleep through the night. I'm not sure I remember what that was like.*

But all those who had been charged with caring for me had apparently been instructed, at some point in their medical training, that patients should never be allowed more than an hour or two of uninterrupted sleep. Every night at about two o'clock, an orderly would come into the room, a young woman bracingly cheerful for that time of night, and ask me to hold out my arm.

"Time to draw some blood!" she would say cheerily.

Soon after that, just as I was ready to doze off again, one of my nurses would appear and make a note of my blood pressure, check my temperature, and ask how bad my pain was. Whenever my expression showed that I was beginning to struggle with the throbbing of stitched abdominal muscle, I was told to push the clicker and gave myself another shot of dilaudid.

"Got to stay ahead of the pain," the nurses always said.

Early every morning, Dr. Lighter would stop in to check my chart and ask how I was doing. His real work with me, he routinely noted, would start once I was released from the hospital.

About a half hour after him, either Dr. Rodriguez or the surgical resident (who often said, "——'s operation was the most interesting one in my training so far") would appear and ask to see what everyone called "my belly." At first they seemed concerned mainly about my incision. After a few days, though, they seemed satisfied that I wasn't developing any infection and that I wasn't likely to tear out any of the staples. But then they started spending more and more time listening to my stomach and intestines. There I'd lie, hospital gown pulled up to my chest, trying to breathe normally with a strikingly cold stethoscope pressed against my abdomen.

"Why do you always want to listen to my stomach?" I finally asked Dr. Rodriguez.

"Well, no one reads about this side of things in medical books or on the Internet because it's not news. It happens to everyone recovering from certain operations. But we have to make sure that your digestive tract is working before we let you go home. The way your incision is coming along, we could sign you out right now. But we can't release you if your intestines are lying inside like a big wet sock. I really had to do some work on you once we had you opened up."

"Work?"

"Pushing and pulling. I pulled your stomach way up, and I pushed your large intestine down and away. And once you touch an intestine, it just stops working. So now we hope for some rumbling. But you're awfully quiet inside. Have you been able to eat anything?"

"I ordered an omelet yesterday morning, and before it came I was actually daydreaming about how good it would taste. But they fried that omelet at least three times too long. It was like chewing on latex. It made me gag, and just thinking about it now makes me want to gag again."

"Maybe try some applesauce or some yogurt. You have to give your system something to work on."

"Are you sure that's the issue? I mean, are you sure there's not something else wrong with me? Did you find something during the operation that no one's talking about?"

"Hold on a second. Just think about what's happened to you. No more of those killer headaches. No more of that explosive heart-pounding. Plus, we're not giving you anything for your blood pressure right now, and it's just about normal. It's a great life, right?"

"That's all well and good. I just can't quite shake the feeling that there's still something nasty growing in me. Month after month, year after year, and I never had a clue I had something inside that could act up and almost kill me. Now I feel like I'm walking around with an implanted time bomb."

Before surgery, I had joked that I wasn't sure how wise it was for a Calvinist to have a Baptist operating on him. Now he got me back:

"You weren't kidding about all that Calvinist stuff, were you? Here you didn't have to do anything more than take a nap on the operating table while I pushed the limits of my skill and gave you a second chance. And you're still looking over your shoulder. Eat something today, and then do some walking around the ward — exercise usually stimulates digestion."

"But, Doc — "

"I don't want to hear it. You've been given a gift. Unwrap it."

∞

"Dad, how far west on 17 did Hubie say it was?" Jon was rotating the partially folded map and checking it from several angles.

"About thirty-five kilometers — twenty miles or so. We're supposed to watch for a shot-up sign for the Shangri-La Motel. Just past the sign is the two-track to the lake."

It was our last day in northwest Ontario, and we were driving to what was known as a musky-action lake, a lake where our fishing camp had boats cached.

"You might not catch a fifty-incher," Hubie had said, sounding a note of caution, "but it's possible for everyone to have some action, and there are some fifty-inch fish in there."

The fact that we would be spending our last day on an action lake had made the boys more noticeably feverish than usual to target muskies. All week long the six of us had kept a careful tally of how many muskies each of us had caught, and the boys had been unable to accept the fact that, going into the last day, I, one of the old guys, was in the lead.

"Something is way off here," Joel said, speaking for all of them late Wednesday night after everyone learned that I had gone into the lead. "Nothing personal against you or Duzzer, really, but there's no way one of you should be beating us. You two really aren't good musky fishermen. Whether you're fishing together or not, half the time you're looking all around, checking out who knows what, and you jabber about everything from junior-high girlfriends to old-time Detroit Tigers we've never heard of. And you hardly ever finish your retrieves with an L-turn. We've seen both of you pull your lures right out of the water when a fish was coming so hot that it ended up almost ramming the boat. Worst of all, every so often you sit down. You can't sit down and fish for muskies!"

"That may all be true," I said, putting on my most irritating tone. "But the world according to you pups is not necessarily the real one. Look around and talk and sit down or whatever, the fact is that the old guys have done just fine so far, thank you very much. I'm in the lead with four, and Duzzer is tied with Jon and Jason with three."

"That's all gonna change. Not tomorrow, when we fly out for walleyes, but for sure on Friday, when we drive to that action lake. What's it called — Stewart Lake? One or more of us will tie you or go ahead on Friday. I guess you already know how to be a gracious loser."

So on Friday morning, knowing that the scorecard could change quickly and dramatically, all four boys were about coming out of their skins with impatience to get to Stewart. "Today's the day," they would repeat, nodding at each other and smirking in my general direction.

"There it is! There's the sign for the motel, and there's the two-track," Jason called out.

"Exactly eighteen-point-six miles," said T-Gunz. "Can you believe this GPS?"

The two-track went directly through two huge puddles and ended in a railroad grade, at the foot of which we left the van nestled between some firs with several fractured limbs.

"Everybody's got to have a life jacket in the boat," I called out to the boys, who had started to lug gear over the grade to the shore. "And this lake's not huge, so we don't all have to stay together, unless you want to. Maybe you guys want to watch Duzz and me catch a few more."

"Dream on," T-Gunz said. "You old guys are on your own today. And you'd better start loading up your boat or we'll have a fish on before you've even shoved off!"

"You guys know how to talk the talk," I yelled back. "But walking's a different thing."

"Now he who limps is talking about walking!" T-Gunz called over his shoulder as he pushed a boat away from shore.

By the time Duzzer and I had our gear arranged in our boat the way we wanted it, both of the boys' boats were floating a couple of hundred yards away, near several boulders heaved up out of the water around what looked to be a miniature and very rusty radio tower.

"They've started in a good-looking spot," I said, pointing to it when Duzzer turned. "But let's motor past them across this lower part of the lake, paddle under the bridge Hubie mentioned, and fish the upper section. I hear there's some great water up there."

"Sounds good to me. You've got the map Hubie drew. I'll steer where you point."

The waves were not nearly as high as they had been our first night back on Eagle; this surface simply had some light chop. As Duzzer headed out at full throttle, we felt a steady thwack, thwack, thwack against the bow.

As we coasted into the narrow channel leading under the bridge, I pressed my face almost to my knees.

"You okay?" Duzzer called. "I was watching to see if you signaled to slow down. You're not oozing, are you?"

"Naw. Just felt a twinge down on the left side for a second. A little reminder, I guess. Look at the territory back here!"

The rocks came down to the shoreline in brazen hues and sharp lines. But in many places, mosses and lichens had worked to soften, to cover the glinting ochres and golds with a bluish green, to carpet the cracks and smooth off the edges.

"It's a whole 'nother world back here," Duzzer said, hushed. "I've got to get some pictures."

"Let's hope we'll be getting some shots of good fish, too," I said as I snapped on what I regarded as my secret weapon. The night before, after we had flown back from Oak Lake, I had spent some time on the dock talking to a group of guys from northern Wisconsin. They had told me that anglers trying for muskies on Stewart Lake could use any lure they wanted so long as it was a Buchertail spinner with an orange blade and a black skirt. "Don't even think about taking it off," they had repeated. I just happened to have a Buchertail in those colors, and as I snapped it on my leader, I reminded myself to stay patient with it, to trust that it would produce sooner or later.

I did leave that lure on throughout the morning and into the afternoon, even though it was frustrating to use. After almost every cast I had to retrieve it three or four feet and jerk on the line several times before the blade would start to spin. And then when I would start to draw the spinner into an L-turn at the side of the boat, the blade would stop spinning and lie with just the slightest wobble against the shaft. I was wasting a good part of nearly every retrieve. I checked the spinner repeatedly, once even using my pliers to try to straighten out what looked like a slight bend in the shaft; but the lure never performed as it was supposed to. And as Duzzer and I fished our way along the shorelines of several parallel finger coves gouged out of shield rock, I had no strikes and no follows.

Something must have put them off their bite today, I mused, reminding myself that Duzzer hadn't seen a thing either.

As we emerged from the last of the finger coves, I turned to Duzzer.

"What do you think? Want to stay up in this part of the lake, or do you think we should go back and check on the boys?"

"We'd better touch base with them," he said. "Not that they won't be all right on their own, but maybe they've figured something out that we're missing. We've got a little time before we have to pack up, don't we?"

"A little — maybe forty-five minutes or so."

We headed back to the lower part of the lake, but after we had paddled our way under the bridge, it took us at least a half hour to find the boys. They were back in the easternmost bay of the lower section of the lake, easily the worst-looking water I had seen all day.

"Why in here?" I called as Duzzer cut the engine and we coasted toward the boys' boats. "This whole bay looks to be only three or four feet deep. Plus the bottom seems coated with orange slime, and there are just a few scraggly weeds here and there."

"Dad, look over there," Jason said, quietly insistent. "See those regular-sized lily pads? Not the silver-dollar pads. The big ones."

"Yeah. What about them?"

"Watch this." He then cast his baby loon Top-raider slightly beyond the cluster of four lily pads, and as the lure clacked its way past the weeds, a wake rose from among the lilies and swelled up behind the twirling blade of the lure.

"There!" Jason exulted. "Shoot, no! Almost. It nipped, but I didn't get a hook into it. Did you hear it?"

"Have you guys had action like that all day?" I asked. Seeing that wake reminded me that I still had one adrenal gland left.

"Yup," Joel yelled as he made a cast. "It looks like terrible water, we know, but it's been a blast. Any time you can find even a small cluster of full-sized lilies and make a good cast to them with a surface lure, the fish have been busting up on it. They're not all huge — mostly around thirty-five inches — and they don't all get on or stay on the hook, but those that we've hooked go nuts. Jason had one almost knock itself out when it jumped and hit the engine. We've been busy almost all day. Both Jon and Jason are up to four fish for the week now. And T-Gunz and I have added one each to our count. How about you guys? What are your numbers?"

I knew they would catch any attempted deception on my part: "Same as they were this morning. We haven't seen a thing."

They all turned directly toward us.

"Aha!" said Joel, the first to gloat. "So you're no longer in the lead, huh? Jason and Jon have tied you. It's exactly what we predicted. So how does it feel?"

"Don't get all worked up. We saw plenty of great-looking water in the upper part of the lake. We just couldn't call up any fish. I probably shouldn't have kept this spinner on all day."

"What is that?" Jason had pulled off his polarized sunglasses. "A Shumway?"

"No, it's a Buchertail. Last night some guys on the dock back at Eagle, guys who I assumed had been up here a lot, told me this would slay the fish in Stewart. But I don't like the way this thing runs — or doesn't run. Pooch your boats over this way a second and I'll show you. Maybe you guys can tell me what's wrong with this lure."

After they moved closer, I dropped the spinner a couple of feet into the water between our boat and theirs.

"Now watch," I said as I pulled the lure toward the surface and then let it settle back into the bay. "See? The blade doesn't always start spinning when this thing comes through the water. Cast after cast today, I had to do all kinds of confounded jerking on the line to get this thing spinning, and it would often flat-out stop when I started my L-turn. Here — watch one more time."

I gave the spinner another pull, and in the first inch of its upward motion, a fish flashed out from under our boat, flared its gills, engulfed the spinner, turned with the bait back toward our boat, felt some tension in the line, slashed to the surface, churned up a boil, dove back under our boat, suddenly reversed direction and erupted out of the water once, then again, and then again so violently that it did a twisting somersault in the air before it hit Duzzer above the knees and fell into the half-inch of muddy water in the bottom of the boat, where it used its tail in an apparent attempt to dent the hull.

"Stop it!" Duzzer yelled, and to avoid being pelted with any more droplets of boat-bottom water, he reached down and grabbed the fish behind the neck, managing to keep most of its body still. "When I say stop it, I mean stop it!" he added as punctuation to the chaos of the past few seconds.

"What is it? What kind of fish?" Jason looked ready to jump up and try to balance on his boat's narrow gunnel.

"Not sure yet," I said. "Here, Duzz, let me get a hold of it. Yes sir, I suspected when it came out of the water like that, but now I can see for a fact — it's a musky." Then I reached for my pliers and started working on the hooks, which were deep in the cartilage of the fish's jaw.

"It's not the biggest musky in all the world," I said to the boys, "probably only thirty-three inches or so, but it is a musky, and according to the rules we all agreed to, every musky counts. This one goes on the scorecard. And since it's time to head in, I guess you know who the grand-prize winner for the week is."

"You can't be serious," Jason said. "You weren't even fishing. You were just messing around, jerking that lure next to the boat and complaining that it didn't spin. Where's the skill in that? Plus, you never even really landed that fish — it just jumped in the boat. It probably would have jumped right over the boat if Duzzer hadn't been in the way. That was a fluke!"

"You all think that?" I asked as I held the fish over the side to revive it.

They all murmured their agreement with Jason.

"Well, there's no way I'm gonna let you guys mess with my head. I caught this musky, I'm gonna count it, and I'm gonna savor its memory. I've been working on learning new lessons, so now I'm trying to unwrap everything."

"Dad," one of my sons responded — I was watching the musky gradually submerge and wasn't sure which boy it was — "unwrapping what? What are you talking about? You can say what you want to when you teach, I guess. But this is fishing. You have to talk sense."

"I am. It's the best sense of my life." ✿

One in a Million

It was late on a Friday night when I reminded Wanda of a promise she had made to me several years earlier.

"Do you remember," I asked, "that all the boys are driving down to Ann Arbor tomorrow to spend the day with T-Gunz? I think there's a Michigan-Indiana soccer game."

"Sure I do," she said. For years she had made notes on the refrigerator calendar about their schedules, and even though the boys were mostly on their own now and didn't stop in every day, she still made as many of those notes as she could. "And you know I check that calendar every night before we go to bed."

"And do you also remember that I was hoping to get out to Murray Lake tomorrow for some musky hunting?"

"I wouldn't call that difficult to remember. Somehow you managed to mention it or drop a hint about it every day this week."

"Okay, I guess that's true. But I wonder whether you remember what you said to me when the boys were little and wanted me to take them out in the boat fishing practically every day."

"I'm sure I said a bunch of things. Which one do you mean?"

"I mean what you said about coming out with me yourself. You promised that when the boys were older and weren't available to fish with me, you'd step in as my fishing partner. The boys are a lot older now, and tomorrow none of them will be able to go with me. So I was hoping you would."

"Do you need help launching the boat or something?"

"No, that's no sweat. It's just that I like to have another person in the boat with me. That way someone can net my fish and take pictures of me holding them. Plus, even though fishing is the single biggest part of my life that I've wanted to share with you, I don't remember the two of us fishing together in years."

I wasn't exaggerating. It was true that when our three sons were really young, Wanda and I would often take them out to Myers Lake in the summer, especially the early summer, and help them try for bluegills and sunfish. I would rig up small fiberglass rods and lines with bobbers, tiny sinkers, small hooks, and chunks of nightcrawlers. Then all five of us would take off our shoes and socks and wade several feet into the water, from which point Wanda and I would help the boys make casts out ahead of them into four or five feet of water.

If everything had worked out the way it was supposed to and we could have gotten them set up and focusing steadily on their bobbers, then I could have rigged up one rod for Wanda and another one for me, and we could have said that we were actually fishing together, even though I probably would have set Wanda up to try for panfish and myself to cast shallow-running crankbaits for bass.

But if you have ever tried to take several young boys fishing at the same time, you can probably guess some of the ways in which our fishing excursions got messed up. More than once, especially after he had landed a fish, one of the boys would start hopping from one foot to the other in the water, and I would at first assume it was hopping caused by the excitement of the catch. But then Wanda and I would hear that son actually say he had to "go potty." The two of us would insist that he leave the water and walk all the way over to the bathroom, and the son would insist that one or the other of us walk along with him and wait outside the door until he was finished.

More than once, one of the boys, putting all of his upper-body strength into the sudden move from backcast into cast, would hook one of his brothers in the sleeve of a T-shirt or even — on one grim evening — in the tricep, though not so deeply as to bury the barb in the flesh. Then Wanda or I would have to back both of them to shore, keep them from breaking into a fight, rummage through the tackle box for a pair of forceps, and perform some minor surgery.

And fairly often, when one or more of the boys were back on the shore with us, they would spot leopard frogs hopping along the shoreline. And then Wanda and I, just to make sure they wouldn't chase fleeing frogs into some mucky hole or stretch of shoreline littered with goose droppings, would have to walk behind them. Sometimes, when they insisted on help, we would have to get down on hands and knees and try to herd the leaping frogs toward the flexing traps of our sons' hands.

So it would really be a stretch to say that when Wanda and I took the boys to Myers Lake, the two of us had a chance to fish together.

And things didn't get any better after I bought the boat. On the afternoon when I towed it home from the dealership and wheeled it into the garage, the boys burst from the house and swarmed into the boat, opening compartments, fiddling with the radio, trying to figure out how to turn the fish finder on, tooting the horn, rocking the steering wheel back and forth, and even trying to unlatch the trolling motor and swing it down over the side. And they begged me to pack up our fishing gear and take them out to some nearby lake already that night.

I can't say for certain, but I have always suspected that as Wanda watched our boys manically exploring my trailered boat and listened to them begging me to take them out to some lake, she came to several conclusions, probably all justified: that with three or two or even one of them in the boat, there would be little room — little comfortable room — for her; that an excursion with them on some river or lake was almost certain to involve more rocking and rolling and near capsizing than anything else; and that once they were casting lures with hooks attached, they would probably be downright dangerous to anyone nearby. Whether I'm correct about her thinking or not, it's a fact that it was shortly after the time I first brought my boat home that Wanda said she would let the boys and me do our thing on the water.

Even during the few times that Wanda traveled with the boys and me to fishing camps in the U.P. or Ontario, she spent most of her time on docks or in rented cottages, not in the boat with us. But she repeatedly promised that she would fish with me once the boys were no longer available as partners — maybe in fifteen or twenty years.

Those years had passed, and that was the promise I was reminding her of.

"How long do you plan to stay out at Murray Lake?" she asked. "I have some errands that I absolutely have to take care of tomorrow."

"I know. We don't have to go out all day long. Part of the day would be fine with me. How about if we both run errands in the morning and early afternoon and then head out to Murray Lake around three? Maybe fish for three or four hours. Afterwards we can stop someplace for supper."

"I guess that would work. But are you sure you want to go musky fishing?"

"Sure. Why do you ask?"

"Well, for one thing I haven't used any kind of reel in years. I'm not sure I'll be able to handle one of those baitcast reels you guys use for muskies."

"They're easy. I can adjust them so it'll be practically impossible for you to have any backlashes. It'll take me about two minutes to show you how to work them right."

"Maybe so, but you realize that I'm probably not going to be able to cast for hours and hours straight. Those rods are huge, and some of the lures I see lying around the basement must weigh at least a pound."

"More like half that."

"That's still too much for me to throw for any length of time. I'm going to have to take plenty of breaks and just enjoy the scenery. The trees are in good color right now, and I hear there are some gorgeous homes on Murray."

"That's fine. Take all the breaks you want. At least part of the time we'll have more than one lure in the water. And just be ready to grab the net when I get a hit."

"You realize that the boys often give me reports about how successful you guys are when you go out, and unless I've got things mixed up, whenever you go musky fishing, you don't seem to have nearly as much action as you do when you go for pike or bass. Your numbers are lower — almost always, I think. A musky or two, maybe three on an absolutely great day. And your numbers are never that low when you go for bass or pike. I remember after one trip to Miner Lake, the boys came crashing into the house all worked up. They were excited because the four of you had caught ninety-six bass that day, mostly good ones, they said. They were all upset because they wanted to stay and get a hundred. But I guess you said it was time to leave."

"Yeah, that's true. I was never too comfortable fishing after dark with them when they were young, and by the time we had caught those ninety-six bass, the sun had set."

"Another time you went to Muskegon Lake. I think it was you, Jon, and Jason. And you got somewhere around thirty-five pike."

"Thirty-six. Jon got twenty, Jason got eleven, and I got five. All from the deep weed edge extending to the east from the state park launch."

"Thirty-five or thirty-six — that's a lot of pike."

"Yup, that was one of our best pike days ever. But what's your point?"

"Well, it really doesn't make that much difference to me since I'll probably want to spend a good part of my time checking out the scenery. But as long as we're going, wouldn't you rather try for bass or pike and not muskies? You'd almost certainly have a lot more action."

"Musky fishing's super tough, no doubt about that. Sometimes those fish can be downright maddening. Just about everybody says they're the fish of ten thousand casts. The way my elbow and rotator cuff have been feeling lately, I'd say they're the fish of a million casts. A couple of times this past spring, Jason and I put in ten- or twelve-hour days of hard fishing, and we never hooked or saw a single fish. Sometimes the boys and I see them following two or three feet behind our lures, lazy-like, as if they're just curious, and as we get the lures close to the boat, they just make a tantalizingly slow turn away from us and disappear. Sometimes we don't see a thing until our lure is a foot or two from the side of the boat, and then one will flash out from under the boat and right past the lure and be gone — so fast, like a glint of light, that you wonder afterwards whether you actually saw a fish or not. One time up at Eagle Lake, Joel had a big one — probably at least a forty-eight-incher — follow his in-line spinner around the figure eight about ten times. Joel said he actually brushed the Flashabou on that spinner's tail against the beast's snoot two or three times, but he couldn't get it to open its mouth."

"I've heard the boys mentioning follows," Wanda said, "usually in arguments about who's had the most."

"Yeah, and the frustration doesn't always end there. Sometimes muskies actually hit the lure, but it's just a nip or a tonk, enough to make us set the hook, but then nothing's there. And even when they get on the hook, they have dozens of ways to get off, mainly by going airborne and shaking their heads like mad in midair, which can send the lure flying back at you."

"Well, as I said, it doesn't make a world of difference to me, but if muskies are so tough to catch, why do you guys keep trying for them?"

"When the effort finally pays off, it pays off big-time. If you're only gonna make a few casts tomorrow, it probably won't happen to you. But if you were to fish hard enough to tie into a musky, the strike and fight would probably be one of the most intense experiences of your life."

"Spoken by someone who has never given birth."

"Well, all right, all I know about that comes from helping you do that special breathing. But when it comes to fishing, I don't know how you can beat musky action."

"The best action there is?"

"The best in freshwater, at least in my opinion. Every one of the boys could tell you more than one wild story. One time along the north shore of Murray Lake, Jon made a cast with a beat-up old black-and-white Burt that he loved, and the second that lure hit the water a musky, about forty inches, was on it. Leaping and shaking its head, leaping again and shaking its head, going subsurface hard for fifteen or twenty feet, then leaping and shaking its head a third time, and that's when the Burt came flying back at us and got snagged in the sleeve of my wool shirt. Good thing I had that heavy old shirt on."

"So he lost the fish?"

"Yeah, but he got another one about the same size later that night. But that leaper was so wild I'm sure he remembers that fight to this day. Another time, just west of the sunken island in Murray, Jason started fooling around with this large firetiger Suick he got at a lure swap. He retrieved it after a long cast and then said that maybe we should all start trying wilder figure eights. 'Like this,' he said, laughing as he started drawing that Suick through the water, giving it a really sharp jerk every foot or so, his rod making loud swishing noises through the water. And then, do you know what happened?"

"No," Wanda said, "but I have a feeling you're going to tell me."

"Some fish he had no clue was anywhere around came flashing out from under the motor, T-boned the Suick and impaled itself on the hooks, immediately started trying to shake the lure but couldn't, and then started taking drag as it dove straight down out of sight. Jason had his drag set as high as it could go, and that fish was still ripping off line — zeet, zeet, zeet, zeet. But he eventually turned it and got it in the net."

"So he was just fooling around and a fish hit?"

"Right. A lot of people fool around in a boat, but he was fooling around with a lure in the water. Actually I think something like that has happened to him more than once. He just does figure eights, or tries something new on a figure eight, and some fish appears out of nowhere and nails his lure. When that happens, it can really get your pulse going. It's like everything is tranquil and then an M-80 explodes next to the boat."

"Do muskies always come as such a surprise?"

"Quite often. Remember that forty-four-incher I got about a month ago?"

"You mean the one you called everyone you know to tell about it?"

"Yup. That one almost gave me a heart murmur. Jason and I had been at it on Murray for about two hours and we hadn't seen a thing. I had tossed just about everything I like to use — a Little Claw, a Mag Dawg, a Triple D, a Shumway Flasher. And then we decided to fish the A-frame shoreline and I switched to a Suzy Sucker. It looks just like a nine-inch sucker but it has a flat tail perpendicular to its body, and that tail flaps hard from side to side when you retrieve it. So I made this long cast with Suzy, gave her several sharp pulls as I reeled her in, got her to boatside and was doing this really smooth figure eight. But I didn't see anything. So I left Suzy a couple of inches below the surface as I hit the trolling motor to move closer to a swimming dock. Then, straight from below the lure this huge open mouth appeared — it was like a scene from *Jaws* or something — and absolutely engulfed Suzy. It was all so fast and startling that I could hardly process what was happening. But somehow my body went on autopilot and I stood up, gave about the hardest hookset I've managed in my life, and held that fish as it turned and dove under the boat. I landed that fish, but even now I can hardly remember all the details of the fight. I just keep seeing that huge mouth appearing from directly below and swallowing Suzy."

"I'm not sure I'd want to be sitting quietly in a boat and have that happen to me," Wanda said. "I startle pretty easily, you know."

"It doesn't always happen like that. Sometimes you get a little warning. One drizzly afternoon Joel and I were out together. I think we were the only ones on Murray that day. I was keeping the boat about fifteen yards off the edge of one of the shallow points. That way I could fish a deep diver off the edge, and Joel could toss a Weagle, which is really a big walk-the-dog lure, up over the weeds on the point. You give your line sharp downward twitches with your rod tip, and the Weagle goes left, then right, then left, then right again. And as it does, it moves a lot of water — goosh, goosh, goosh, goosh. So, even though I was facing away from Joel and his lure, I could hear him working that lure across the point. And then I heard his voice. 'Here comes one,' he said. And I turned, scanned the water, and finally saw half of this big tail sticking out of the water and coming up on his Weagle. For four or five seconds nothing happened. And then there was this large swirl in the water, then another swirl, then an enormous splash — almost like someone dropped a bowling ball in the lake — and Joel yelled, 'Got 'im, got 'im, I got 'im!' That fish swam straight at the boat and then curved away behind the motor and headed for deep water. As it passed us, it was the coolest thing to see because there was almost four feet of musky with Joel's Weagle sideways in its mouth."

"Did you land it?"

"Yup. By the time Joel pumped that thing back toward us from the deep water, it had burned up a lot of energy, and he was able to get its head up pretty well and lead it to me."

"It's neat to hear some of what happens when you go out with the boys," Wanda said. "Since they've gotten older, once they get back to our house and unload their gear, they sometimes take off so fast I don't get more than a few words from them. Maybe you'll hook a fish or two today, and I'll be able to see what all the drama is like for myself."

"Maybe?"

On the road to the lake the next day, I made two decisions, both aimed at helping Wanda see some musky action. The first was to fish only those spots on Murray that had shown the boys and me some consistent action in the past, spots we even had names for: "The Dinner Table," "The Knuckle," "The A-Frame," "The Gate," and "Death Row." The second decision was to skip doing on this trip what I usually did, that is, spending some time trying out a new lure or two. I would stick with what had been working lately: most effective for me had been my copper-colored Little Claw for shallow water and my Walleye Triple D for deeper water.

I let Wanda use one of our shorter musky rods, a seven-foot St. Croix. And I thought that she would enjoy fishing a Crane twitchbait. It was probably the lightest lure I had, but if you gave it even slight twitches as you retrieved it, it would wiggle tightly and throw off lots of vibrations into the water.

As we moved from spot to spot, Wanda did exactly what she had said she would. When we came up to a spot, she would make a few casts; after that she would put her rod down and rest it against the stern. And then she, during her first time ever on Murray Lake, noticed things that I hadn't seen in dozens of prior trips: a wood-duck box in the trees on the west side of the knuckle cove; a wind-worn Mandela hanging from a rusty dock post; and a triangular section of multihued stained glass at the peak of a dormer window.

All the while I fished hard, moving through each spot in one direction fishing the shallow water, and then turning and heading back in the opposite direction fishing deep. But I couldn't make anything happen. I didn't see a single follow. There were never any swirls by my lure when it landed. Not once did a musky swipe at my lure as I brought it through an L-turn at the side of the boat. And I had nothing, not even a momentary snag in subsurface weeds that resembled a hit.

By the time we got to the Dinner Table, the next-to-last spot I was planning to fish, I was feeling a little irritated. I knew all too well that musky fishing could be like deer hunting, that you could wait hours and hours with no action whatsoever, perhaps struggling to keep your hopes from eroding, and then suddenly see what you'd been waiting to see and have an adrenaline rush that would leave you panting, with knees so wobbly that you had to look for a good place to sit down. But since I was eager to show Wanda some example of the wild action I had raved about the night before, I was becoming impatient. "Frustrating fish!" I muttered under my breath.

"Bill," she said.

"Huh? Whew, you startled me a bit. What is it?"

"Look over there. That big house with the tan siding. See it? The one with the wraparound deck."

"Yeah, I see it. What about it?"

"Have you ever counted how many windows that house has? It's unbelievable. Thirty-six that I can see, most of them facing south."

"I've noticed that house before, mainly because it's huge and sits right in the middle of ancient shoe-box cottages, but I've never paid much attention to its windows. You thinking about windows like that for our retirement house?"

"I'm sure we'll never be able to afford windows like that."

"Oh, I don't know. A lot depends on whether you want to keep our house in Grand Rapids. We probably could afford a few special things if we sold that and put everything into a retirement place. Whoa! Hold still, hold still." I immediately brought my voice down. "Don't move! That is just plain unbelievable."

"What?"

"Shush, shush. Just hold as still as you can and turn your head slowly so that you can see behind the motor. See it?" From my seat high in the front of the boat, I had a better angle than she did.

"Oh, you can't. . . . Huh? When did that happen?"

"See it?"

"I see it, I see it. But what is it?"

"That's a musky, a pretty good one, too. Just don't do anything to scare it off."

Wanda had rested her rod against the stern, but she hadn't reeled up the Crane. She had left it wiggling along a few inches below the surface and five or six feet behind the boat. And now, about six inches below the surface and only two inches behind that lure, finning along at exactly the same speed as the boat was being pushed by the breeze, was a musky, about three feet long, eying the Crane intently.

"What should I do? What do you want me to do?" Wanda's voice was a little raspy.

"Easy, now, easy. You're gonna love this. In a second I want you to pick your rod up as quietly as you can. Don't knock it against anything. And try not to change the angle of the line running out the back, so you don't affect what the lure's doing. Then, when you're ready, give that Crane a short jerk, just four or five inches worth. It will twitch, and when it does, if I know anything at all about muskies, that fish is going to slam it. When you can feel the weight, set the hook. You'll be tempted to set the hook when you see the fish make its move toward your lure, but don't set it until you actually feel the fish."

"Set the hook?"

"Jerk it back toward you, hard. You've got to drive the hooks into the fish's jaw. That fish is close, and it's a pretty good one, so when it hits, everything's going to get crazy, but don't panic. Hold on tight and you'll land it. You've got good equipment there, and I checked the drag when we started. Ready?"

"I don't know about this," she said. "You sure you don't want to come back here and do this yourself? The biggest fish I can remember catching was an eight-inch bluegill at Myers Lake."

"No, no, no — this is your fish. You're gonna love it."

"I don't know about this. But here goes."

Wanda picked up her rod slowly, taking care not to scrape it against the stern or knock it against the motor. She glanced once at me and then gave the Crane a sharp jerk, a bit more than I had asked for, but the Crane dove an inch or two and wiggled wildly through ten or twelve inches of water, exactly like a wounded baitfish trying to escape predatory jaws. The second the Crane stopped its wild wiggle, the musky flared its gills, opened its mouth, smashed the rear half of the lure, turned, and when Wanda set the hook, swirled heavily on the surface and then dove.

"No, no," Wanda yelled, struggling to get a better grip on the St. Croix as it throbbed and arced down after the fish. "I can't hold it, I can't hold it — it's too heavy! Why don't you take this one? Bill, you gotta take this one."

"No way! That's your fish. You nailed it. You really nailed it."

"You gotta help. My forearm hurts."

"Just hold on," I said. "Don't you dare let go. You're all right, you're doing great. It's taking drag. Hear that? That's the way it's supposed to work."

"But I can't hold it."

"You'll hold it just fine."

"No way."

"Yes, way. Maybe move your left hand up higher on the rod. That'll give you more leverage."

"Like this?"

"Yeah. But don't touch the line! Around the rod but under the line — there."

"That burns."

"Lucky you let go. Let the drag do the work."

"But now that drag sound stopped . . ."

"All right, it's time," I said. "The beast stopped its run. Try to pump it up this way." I was on my knees in the front of the boat, shoving tackle boxes behind me. Then I stood up, grabbed the net, moved as close to the gunnel as I could, and saw that Wanda had managed to get her line over on my side of the boat.

"Beautiful," I shouted. "You're doing fantastic."

"Phooey! It feels like this thing could pull me in."

"No swimming allowed right now. I'll stay up here, out of your way but still within reach with the net. So see if you can coax that thing toward me."

"It's hardly moving. It feels like I'm hooked to a telephone pole."

"Just keep the pressure on. Pump it up and toward me."

"I'm trying, I'm trying."

"Just a little harder now. You can rest your arms all the way home. See if you can lead it toward me. I'm ready with the net."

"I don't see anything yet," she said.

"I saw a flash down there a second ago," I said. "But now — nothing. Oh, wait. Maybe, maybe. I think I saw its side. Yeah, there it is. Not too far down. We're gonna get this fish, Wanda, we're gonna get it!"

"After all this, we better."

And then that fish rocketed out of the water, curled and twisted in the air so that it came at me sideways, glancing off my left shin and thunking into the bottom of the boat, where it flopped furiously trying to dislodge the hooks.

In an effort to keep it from beating itself unconscious or rubbing off any more protective scale slime than it already had, I slid the edge of the net under the musky, lifted the net as the fish flopped itself deep down into the cords, and then put the bag of the net and the enclosed musky over the side into the water.

"You did it, Wanda, you did it. This baby's yours. Your first musky! What a great job!"

"I can't believe it," she said. "I've got to sort out what just happened. That was all too fast." She had put down her rod and was leaning back in the seat in the rear.

"Once I get the hooks out, you gonna wanna hold this thing while I snap a picture or two?"

"Are you kidding me? Isn't this the kind of fish that cut Jason's hand all up that one time?"

"That's true, but there's trouble only if you relax your grip or get a little careless under the gill plate."

"No way I'm gonna pick that thing up."

"Okay, then let's get a picture of it in the net. Come up here. I'll leave the lure in the corner of its mouth, raise the fish within the frame of the net to the surface and hold it level, and then you snap a couple."

Wanda took her camera out of its bag and moved up to kneel close to me on the left. She leaned out over the edge, framed the fish, and hit the shutter.

"That's really cool," she said as she leaned back and examined her work. "You can see most of the lure and all but the end of the tail. Its eyes are huge!"

"Take a couple more. The boys are gonna be jealous when they see these."

When she was finished, she stowed her camera back in its bag and knelt next to me again, draping an arm over my shoulders and watching intently as I worked the hooks out of the musky's jaw.

"Breathing pretty heavy, aren't you?" I said, chuckling.

"I guess. I hadn't really noticed."

"So what do you think of musky fishing?"

"Well, you were right about one thing."

"What's that?"

"You said musky fishing is intense," she said, "and now I see what you mean. Do I ever see what you mean. But — "

"But what?"

"You were way off with that bit about a million casts." ☞

Memory as Grace

As I drove through Storm Lake, which finally put us only about an hour from our destination in the northwest corner of Iowa, my eyes caught the glint of the low sun on choppy water off to my left, and I turned toward Jason in the back seat.

"I didn't watch when you finished packing your stuff this morning. Did you bring any fishing gear along?"

"Left it all home this trip."

"You did? I know you're twenty-one and all grown up and everything, and Mom and I are really glad that at least one of you boys was able to make the annual summer trip with us, but what are you going to do with yourself all week, especially when we're visiting Grandma at the nursing home? I don't think it's the best idea for you just to lie around Uncle Stan and Aunt Judy's basement and watch ESPN all the time. When you were little, all you ever wanted was for me or Grandpa to take you out to the ponds at Sandy Hollow."

"After getting up early all summer so far for that rec job, I want to sleep in some this week. But I won't just lie around all day watching TV. I definitely want to spend some time out at Sandy Hollow. I'll be able to use the van now and then, won't I? Haven't been to Iowa in five or six years now, and I want to check if Grampa's sandbar is still there, the one where he'd plunk down on his folding chair, rock back and forth to get himself level in the sand, rig up his fishing rod, and then toss his bait out as far as he could. Plus, I want to see if some of the passageways through the tall grass to the shore of the ponds are still there. I even want to check if some of the logs I used to crawl out on to cast into deep water are sturdy enough to hold me now."

"I've never seen anyone more excited about catching fish than you were in those days. Any kind of fish — bluegills, perch, sunfish, catfish, bass. Grampa used to tell me how he loved watching you work your way around those ponds. You'd trot along the high bank, disappear into the puckerbrush, pop out in a small clearing along the water, start to fancast from there, and usually quite soon after that he'd see the splash of a fight."

"The best was when Grampa and I'd have contests. We'd set a time limit, like twenty-five minutes. Then I'd head out while Grampa stayed in his folding chair on his sandbar. One time I caught and released five bass, and I thought I was creaming him. But when I trotted back around to his side of the pond, just as I got close to him, he reached down and lifted his stringer with at least a dozen bluegills on it. So then we have this big debate about whether winning should depend on total numbers of fish or total weight of fish or total length of fish — issues we had forgotten to get straight in the first place. As I think about it now, I don't even remember what we finally decided. One thing's for sure: I don't want to forget anything more about those days. I want to go back and spend some time walking around those ponds to make sure all the memories I still have don't get fuzzy."

"I know," I said. "Those memories are important."

"Without them, I don't think I could stand it that Grampa died."

"I think I understand what you're saying. But if you're going to spend some time out at Sandy Hollow, why not fish?"

"Well, the answer to that's been pretty clear the last few years," Jason said. "At least it should be."

"It should?"

"Absolutely. Haven't you noticed that I've become a musky fisherman?"

"A musky fisherman? And that's it? I know you like chasing muskies, but they're all you're after now? I like catching muskies, too, when I can manage — who wouldn't? But I'm not going to abandon all my other fish, the bass and pike in the spring and summer, and the steelhead and salmon in the fall. What makes me chuckle a little is that whenever you and your brothers talk about musky fishing, what I mainly hear about is you raising fish, seeing follows, counting swipes at your bait, and keeping track of how many times around the figure eight the fish stay after your lure. All in all, I don't hear as much about actually hooking and landing fish. If you just want to see fish, why not buy a DVD or two?"

"We do stick one pretty regularly, you know. But you're getting at one of the things I love most about musky fishing — the challenge. On a couple of our trips to Eagle Lake, I've put in more than one thirteen-hour day trying to catch a single musky. And I bet that I could go out to Sandy Hollow tomorrow and catch a bunch of bass in half an hour or so. One time, when it was drizzly and no one was around, I figured out that the bass were all tucked up under the floating gunk along the shore of the swimming-hole pond. So I walked around the whole pond, stopping every once in a while to cast my Baby One-minus as close to parallel to the shore as I could. I was reeling that lure through ten or twelve inches of water and bass would dart out from under the gunk and smack the lure. I caught two dozen of them in about forty minutes. But you know what? After a while it almost seemed too easy. And the same thing's true for panfish over there. I could dig up some worms and get set up on Grampa's sandbar and catch a stringer-full of bluegills in no time, an hour tops. Where's the challenge in that?"

"I think having just about any fish on the line is fun," I said.

"Sure, but the fish you catch at Sandy Hollow, even the bass, aren't all that big. Especially if you're not a little kid anymore. I think the best I've gotten out of there is sixteen- or seventeen-inch bass. Now my main goal as a fisherman is to nail a musky fifty-three or -four inches long. And I've been getting closer. The one I got this past June, that spotted beast that I drew off an underwater rock column and that then disappeared before flashing out from under the boat when I was on the second loop of my figure eight, was forty-seven inches. Joel and Duzzer and Cal, the guide, were in the boat with me as that fish went nuts, and every single one of us got soaked. I'm looking for more fish like that and bigger fish than that. No more little fish for me! That's why all my equipment stayed home."

"Mom wasn't too good this morning. I haven't been out here in months, but that's probably the worst I've ever seen her. She was awfully tired and kept drifting off. And her short-term memory

— my goodness, Judy, her short-term memory seems just about gone. She'd ask, 'Are you staying by Judy?' Then she'd ask something about the boys. Then it was 'Are you staying by Judy?' all over again. Every two minutes I'd hear the same question. I stayed patient with her, but it was hard. It's so hard."

The day after our long drive, Wanda was back after an early-morning visit with her mother in the nursing home, and I had joined her and her sister Judy in Stan and Judy's main-floor kitchen for breakfast.

"Did she say anything about Dad?" Judy asked, sounding as though she already knew the answer.

"Not at first, but she started up after a while. And she had everything all mixed up. Sometimes she talks as if Dad is in the hospital in Sioux City. Sometimes she mentions that he should be getting out of the rehab home in a day or so and that then they can finally decide on the kind of carpet they want in the living room of the house in Sioux Center they moved into after leaving the farm. Sometimes she says that Dad is late and must be helping Bud combine. Sometimes she says that Dad's in South Dakota to buy some calves. And then she remembers he's dead, and she seems to fold in on herself. When she realizes I'm still in the room with her and says something to me again, she sounds mad at God, which is totally unlike everything I remember about her. I would never have thought it possible for her to talk like that. She just doesn't understand why she has to go on without Dad, why she has to be here alone. And she thinks she isn't any use to anybody anymore. 'Why can't God just take me?' she asks over and over."

"It's an awful thought to have," Judy said, clearing her throat. "But you do have to wonder why God lets some people linger. On most days I wouldn't exactly say that Mom is lingering, but there's one man down the hall from her who just lies on his back in bed all day, every day, with a folded towel over his eyes. And he moans and moans and moans. They usually keep the door of his room shut, but you can't help but hear him when you walk past. You have to wonder how that is part of the plan. And maybe you start to wonder what kind of plan it is."

Wanda glanced at me, and there was a clear message in her eyes, for Judy almost certainly wasn't expressing everything that was on her mind, all those questions we knew she would probably always carry with her about the accidental deaths of two of her children, the baby daughter because of flaming charcoal, the adolescent son because of a careening pickup. Wanda focused again on Grandma:

"I just hope we can get Jason to visit her once or twice. He was so bad when he saw Dad in that bed in the Sioux City rehab home that he started to hyperventilate. After that one short visit, we never could get him back there for another one."

"But Mom's place is nothing like that one," Judy replied. She emphasized her point with quick hand stabs. "It's brand new. All the attendants are cheerful and just about jumping out of their own skin with energy. And as I mentioned, they usually keep the doors shut on the rooms with really troubled residents."

"How about the smell?" Wanda wondered. "That pee smell in the hallways of Dad's rehab home just about wiped Jason out before we even got to Dad's room."

"Mom's place is very clean," Judy said. "In fact, it's immaculate. No dust, no mud, no grime, no smelly stuff. Overall, it's a gorgeous place — you should see all those oak cabinets. And it should be gorgeous for the money that comes out of Mom's account to keep her there: forty-three hundred a month, can you believe that! You know, we could show Jason some pictures. I'm sure I have a brochure around here somewhere. I think he might even like the place."

"What a dreamer you are," Wanda sighed.

"I thought Mom and I were gonna have to work a lot harder to get you to come along and visit Grandma." Later that day Jason and I were a few steps behind Wanda in a bright corridor in the Wildflower Wing of the Royale Meadows Nursing Home.

"It wouldn't make much sense to come all the way to Iowa and not see Grandma when she's still alive," Jason said, taking quick glances into the residents' rooms as we passed them. "It's just that I wasn't sure I could come here and not pass out, like I almost did when I saw Grampa. But the brochure that Aunt Judy showed me helped. This is a fancy place. And it helped that Mom said Grandma's not hooked up to any tubes. That tube that Grampa had going right into his chest — yech. Plus, Mom said that no one will come around to stick her in a toe with a needle. You know I can't stand to be around needles."

Wanda turned off the corridor and into a room.

"Wanda! Honey! What a surprise! How nice of you to visit me! This is a special treat."

"Mom, I was here already today, early this morning. I see you've moved into the recliner."

"And here's Bill, too — both of you come all the way from Michigan. Thanks so much, Bill, for bringing Wanda out for a visit. And who is this? Who is this practically hiding in the doorway? Come on in where I can see you — why, it's Jason. Right? It's got to be Jason. So tall now I hardly recognize you! How tall are you? You've grown like a weed in the ditch. My, my, my."

Jason bent low to give his grandma a hug around the neck. "About six foot seven now, Grandma. And I'm probably not done growing. I'm surprised that you still recognize me. It's been a while."

"Oh, I never forget my three grandsons from Michigan, that's for sure. Wanda keeps writing me about them. But Jon and Joel didn't come? No? Too busy, I suppose. Well, maybe next time. But you, I remember when you were so little you could just about fit in a tomato box. But where are you all staying while you're here?"

"Mom," Wanda replied, faster than Jason could, "remember we talked about that this morning? We're staying by Stan and Judy. You know they've fixed up their basement so that guests have their own apartment down there."

"So, Jason," Grandma went on immediately, "you're a teacher, right? A teacher just like your mom and dad. What is it again that you teach?"

"No, Grandma, you must be thinking of one of my brothers — maybe Joel. Joel's a phys-ed teacher. Me, I'm still in college. I've switched majors a couple of times, but now I'm in sports management."

"Sports management? But how can you teach that? You're a teacher, right? I can almost see you in front of a class. So tall you must give everyone a crink in the neck. What do you teach about when you teach sports management?"

"No, Grandma, I'm not exactly sure what I'll do with sports

management after I graduate, but I'm not going to be a teacher."

"Not a teacher? Not a teacher like your mom and dad? That's a surprise. So where are you staying when you're out here?"

"Like Mom said, we're staying by Stan and Judy. Same place we usually stay when we come to Iowa."

"Have you already been out to Sandy Hollow? I remember you used to spend practically all day every day out there exploring those ponds."

"Haven't had a chance yet. But I'm for sure going to get out there, maybe even later today. There's lots of stuff I want to see again."

"Your grandpa's probably out there right now. Before it's time to start combining, he usually tries to get in as much fishing as he can."

"No, Grandma, that can't be."

"Well, then, you must not know your grandpa very well. He'll be there. And it'll be good for him to have some company. I always worry a little about him sitting on the edge of those deep ponds all by himself. 'Course there are people pretty close, all the golfers, but I'm not sure how much attention they pay to anyone sitting by the ponds. And this time of year the weeds around the water will be really high."

"Well, I'm going to check everything out, but I'm not planning to fish."

"Not fish? 'Course you're gonna fish. Dad always brags about how good of a team the two of you make, you running to spots along the shoreline while he holds the fort on his sandbar. I have a picture around here someplace — I wish I could remember where I put it — of the two of you holding up a stringer of beautiful bluegills."

"Mom," Wanda cut in, "when we moved you in here, Judy, Kathy, and I went through all your boxes of pictures with you, picked out some of your favorites for these two wall displays, and stored the rest of them in Stan and Judy's shed. Since that picture's not on the wall, it must be in storage."

"Really? I was sure I had it around here someplace — seems like I just looked at it the other day. I'd love to see it again. Jason, you remember the one I'm talking about, don't you? There were so many fish on the stringer it took both you and your grandpa to lift them. Do you two ever look proud in that picture! And Dad loves bringing home a mess of bluegills for lunch. I think that's his favorite meal. That's it, beans and bluegills. I bet he could have a meal of fresh green beans and bluegills every day. So don't get any funny ideas about not helping him catch some bluegills. We can fill up that freezer in the basement with them if we have to."

"But Grandma, I just don't think that'll work out."

"'Course it'll work out. You've got the time, don't you? What is this, your summer vacation? Your vacation from teaching? A teacher just like your mom and dad. They must be so proud of you. What better time for you to fish than when you're on your summer vacation?"

"Mom," Wanda said, getting up from her chair and tucking the afghan in around Grandma's legs, "let's talk about something other than fishing. With the men I live with, I hear about fishing just about every day."

"Sure, honey. I can see how you'd get tired of talking about fishing. So where are you all staying when you're out here?"

"Time for a change in plans," Jason said, leading Wanda and me down the nursing home hallway away from Grandma's room.

"What do you mean?" Wanda asked. She seemed close to alarm.

"Well, as I was saying on the drive yesterday, I was planning to visit Sandy Hollow and walk around and just check things out. But now I think I should go out there and catch some bluegills."

"How come?" I asked. I was surprised, because once Jason made up his mind about something, he hardly ever changed it.

"Do you guys remember the time after my visit to Grampa in that rehab home, the time when Uncle Stan drove me out to Sandy Hollow in the middle of winter and I chopped a hole in the ice, caught a nice northern, posed with it while Stan took a picture, and then we sent that picture along with you on your next visit to Grampa?"

"Sure." Wanda and I said almost in unison.

"Well, you told me that when Grampa saw the picture of the pike and of me making our sign for the 'first of many more to come,' he really perked up. You said that he was back to his old self for a while. Now after what Grandma said about a picture of bluegills, I'm thinking it might pick her up a little bit if I could get her a picture like that. So tonight, if I can use the van for a while, I'm going to head out to the ponds and catch a stringerful of bluegills."

"It would probably work," I said, "for you to drop Mom and me off here for our visit tonight. We'll probably stay for a couple of hours, so that should give you enough time to catch your fish. You told me that you could catch a bunch in about an hour, right? But now that you've left all your fishing equipment home, how are you going to pull this off?"

"Pretty much the same way I did for the picture for Grampa. I used an old rod that Stan had in his shed — it's probably right where I left it. And there was a small box of hooks and a rusty stringer on a workbench near there, too, I remember. I can easily get some worms out of Judy's garden. I'll ask Stan if I can use that old Polaroid he let me use the last time; I'm guessing he still has it."

"But didn't Stan take the picture of you and the pike? How are you going to take a picture of yourself? I don't think those old Polaroids have a timer." I thought I had discovered the fatal flaw in his plan.

"Easy. I'll just hold the stringer as far away from me as I can in one hand and snap the picture with the other. I used to do that a lot when I was a kid. It works as long as the fish are little. I could never do that with a musky — too big to fit in a picture frame and too heavy to lift."

"Okay, Jase," I said, trying to be helpful. "This might work out. But the last time you ever fished at Sandy Hollow you were young enough to fish without a license. Now you'll need one, I'm sure. Iowa probably has an out-of-state license for a week, maybe for three days. How are you going to get one of those?"

"That's easy, too. After I drop you and Mom off tonight, I'll just swing by the Wal-Mart south of town and pick up the cheapest license they have. Wal-Mart can't be more than five minutes from the nursing home. Then I'll head out and get set up on Grampa's sandbar and catch a bunch of gills. When I'm done, I can hustle back to the nursing home and show Grandma the picture yet tonight."

"I can't really think of anything else, I guess," I said. "But are you sure showing Grandma a picture like that is not going to cause her trouble?"

"Trouble? How could it cause trouble?"

"Don't you think it might confuse her?"

"Confuse her more than she already is? That's what made me think I've got to do something, even like catching a mess of fish I usually wouldn't bother with and showing her a picture of them, so that I can give her a chance to be happy and keep things straight, maybe just for a little while. It just really bugged me that so many of her words didn't match the world, so I'm going to make part of the world match her words."

After dropping Wanda and me off at Royale Meadows that evening and driving off first to get a license and then out to Sandy Hollow, Jason was back leaning against the door frame of Grandma's room after only an hour and fifteen minutes, far sooner than I had expected.

"Something mess up?" I asked from the folding chair nearest the door. "You couldn't buy a license, make it out to Sandy Hollow, and catch a bunch of bluegills in that little time, could you?"

"Oh, yeah! It only took me ten minutes to get a three-day nonresident license at Wal-Mart. And I wasn't blowing smoke when I said I could catch a bunch of bluegills in no time at all. Grampa's sandbar is still there, almost exactly the way it was the last time I ever fished with him, and I caught gills on both sides of it, even in fairly shallow water. I stopped after I got to fifteen. They filled up the stringer."

"And how about the picture you were talking about?"

"Got it. It's a little grainy, but you can still make out the individual fish. And in the background you can see one of those logs I used to crawl out on. The fish stayed really lively on the stringer until I took the picture, and then I released them." He handed me the picture.

The picture was a little fuzzy, but the fish were big enough to make an impressive display, and you could even tell how he had taken the picture, because part of Jason's left forearm was visible extending from the edge of the picture frame to his hand holding the top of the stringer.

"What's that?" Grandma asked from her recliner. "Something secret, or can the rest of us have a peek?"

"Oh," said Jason, "I went out to Sandy Hollow and took a picture. Sure, you can see it. I took it just for you, Grandma. See here? See all the bluegills?" He handed her the picture, and Wanda pulled her folding chair up next to the recliner to see the picture with her mother.

"My, my, my! Just look. Just look at those beautiful bluegills. Those sure are big. What are they, about ten inches?"

"Not quite. Most are eight or nine, Grandma. But they fought pretty hard, harder than I expected."

"Well, you young Michigander, you should know by now that fish out here can really fight. This is Iowa, and these are genuine Ioway bluegills, you know. Homegrown. Ha! Whattaya think — these fish wouldn't fight harder than those you catch back in Michigan?"

"A bluegill's a bluegill, Grandma. It doesn't matter if it lives in Michigan or Iowa."

"It doesn't matter? Did you come all the way out here to try to be funny? Your grandpa always says that a Sandy Hollow bluegill can yank the rod right out of his hand, even if he is paying attention. And I don't think you'd be able to say that about a Michigan bluegill, no I don't. These sure are some beauties. 'Course that's exactly what you'd expect, right?"

"I knew they would be good-looking fish because the ones I caught with Grampa when I was little, before I started going for bass, were good fish. But you can get good ones in Michigan, too. I don't fish for them anymore, but I used to, and they were nice. If you don't believe me, just come along with me sometime to Lincoln Lake. I could show you some monster bluegills there, even bigger than these."

"What? I'm supposed to make a trip all the way to Michigan and then hop in a boat? With my knees? Oh my! Here a daughter of mine gets it into her head to move away after college to Wisconsin, then moves to Illinois and gets married there, then moves to Michigan, and finally has what kind of children? Why, she has children who think they know better than their grandma! Just try to argue with me, I dare you." This was the grandma we all remembered, the sprightly lady who never faced a chore she didn't have the energy for, who was intensely competitive, especially in card and board games, often close to laughter, usually looking for chances to make or prolong a little mischief, certain that no one who had even a small measure of wit would ever want to live anywhere other than Iowa.

"Just a minute, Mom, I need my purse," Wanda said. She got up and walked over to her purse on the windowsill, took out a tissue, and turned out toward a field of soybean plants showing their first touches of gold.

"Sure, honey. Maybe there's something in the air in Judy's

basement that you're a little allergic to." She focused again on Jason's picture. "So who belongs to the arm and hand in the picture, anyway? That's not Dad — his wrist is a lot thicker than that."

"That's my arm, Grandma, can't you tell? Just look at those Michigan muscles."

"But I thought you took the picture."

"I did. The stringer was pretty heavy, but I held it out away from me as far as I could with my left hand and then used my right hand to snap the picture. I've taken lots of fish pictures that way. They're not usually as good as when someone else takes them, but they're better than no picture at all."

"But why didn't your grandpa take the picture?"

"He couldn't, Grandma, he couldn't. I had to do it on my own."

"I'm sure he could manage. Well, he's no expert with cameras and all these newfangled gadgets and stuff, but if you get all the dials set up and then show him what button to press, I know he could do that."

"But I was there by myself."

"So where was your grandpa? I was sure he was out at Sandy Hollow fishing. At least before he has to help Bud get the corn in. Why isn't he in the picture? Where is he now?"

"Oh, Grandma," Jason said. "You know, don't you?"

Wanda moved from the window back to the chair next to the recliner, and took her mom's hands in hers.

"It's going to be okay, Mom, it really is. Let's not get all upset now."

"It's going to be okay? What do you mean it's going to be okay? Where's Dad? Why isn't he in the picture? He should be in the picture. I love seeing pictures of him and big fish. He always looks so happy in those pictures that he seems to be floating a little above the ground. I want to know where he is."

"There, there, Mom, it's all right. Don't you remember? That picture — Jason just took it earlier tonight. It wouldn't be possible for Dad to be in that picture. We'll have to look through all your pictures in storage and find one of him holding up some fish."

"Is Dad in the hospital? Did they take him to Sioux City? How come it's so hard for me to understand what the doctors say? He has to have an operation, doesn't he? Some kind of obstruction. Shouldn't we have heard something by now? And how come Reverend Smit hasn't stopped by yet today?"

"He had the operation, Mom," Wanda said. "He already had it. And then he spent all those weeks in that rehab home in Sioux City. Right around the time when the two of you left the farm and moved to town."

"Left the farm? Dad and I left the farm?" And then Grandma looked at Wanda, looked at Jason, looked at me, and then looked out the window, perfect lucidity in her eyes, her lower lip starting to quiver.

"He couldn't have fished with Jason," she said. "He's never going to fish again. No more of those lazy afternoons out at Sandy Hollow. No more meals of bluegills and beans. He's not coming back. He's never coming back. He got through the operation just fine, just fine, they all said. But he was weak, and he hated that rehab home. Never cooped up like that before in his life. And then his kidneys stopped working in Sioux City. Oh, I remember now — I remember all of it. He just rolled on his side during dialysis and died. Just like that, he rolled over and stopped breathing. It was almost like he was saying it was all too much. Oh, Bill, my Bill — he's not coming back to me ever again, is he? I miss him. That's all I can do now, I just miss him so much. Why can't things be the way they were?"

And then, even as Wanda continued to hold her hands securely, she lowered her chin almost to her chest and started to shake, somewhat gently and regularly at first, then almost violently and very sporadically, so that whenever I thought she might be over it, another spasm would rack her body. And then she started to weep, not loudly enough for someone outside in the hallway to hear, but steadily, a soft keening, utterly forlorn.

Wanda let go of her hands and slid one arm behind her so that she could bring her head close to her mother's neck and embrace her.

"There, there, Mom. What did I tell you? What did I tell you? It's going to be all right. Everything's going to be all right. Just imagine the people Dad gets to fish with now. Or the ones he gets to tell fishing stories to. Did you ever think of that? And you always told me we'd all see each other again. You know you said that."

Hearing that just made Grandma shake worse, so hard that it looked as if she might hurt herself. Wanda looked up at me: "Bill, can you come here and see if you can calm her down a little? It's just about time for visiting hours to be over, and we can't leave her this way. I'm going to run out and find an attendant and see whether she can give Mom something to settle her down for the night."

"Let me," Jason whispered to me. "I've got an idea." He took Wanda's chair as she hurried out, folded his grandmother's fingers within his long hands, leaned down close to her left ear, and whispered something.

I was off to her side, so I can't say for sure, but after Jason pulled back from her, the expressions on her face made it look as if she moved through a series of several emotions in about thirty seconds. First she seemed almost angry, then confused, then quizzical or curious, and finally placid. That's when she stopped shaking and turned toward Jason, blinking to clear the tears from her eyes, almost transfixed. "You really think so?" she murmured. "Can it be?"

"I'm sure of it, Grandma," he said. "I'm as sure of it as I'm sure of anything."

"Well," she responded, and pulled her hands from his so that she could reach up, then took him by the shoulders and gave him a little shake. "Well."

"What happened? How did you get her to calm down?" Wanda said as she came back into the room with a young attendant, who hurried over to check Grandma's pulse.

"I'm not exactly sure," I said. "It all happened so fast." I shook my head. "You've got to ask Jason — he's the one who did it."

The attendant spoke up: "Whatever upset her, she seems fine now. You're fine, aren't you, Theresa?"

"Yes," Grandma said. "Not sure what came over me."

"You're fine — I can tell. And I'll help you get ready for bed. She's perfectly all right, folks, so you don't have to worry about leaving her. We'll have some cookies and punch together, I'll read one of her devotionals with her, and then I'll help her get ready for bed. Don't worry, when you see her tomorrow, she'll be as good as new."

"Are you sure we shouldn't stay a while yet?" asked Wanda. "Just to be sure she's okay?" It was clear that she was hesitant to leave.

"No, no, you don't have to worry. The two of us have everything under control. After a snack and our bedtime reading, she'll be ready to sleep like a baby."

"You're sure?" Wanda said. "Okay, so good night, Mom. I'll be back first thing in the morning to see how you're doing. I want to see you as much as I can while we're out here." Wanda kissed her mom good night and then scooched out of the way so that Jason and I, in turn, could give her a hug.

As the three of us walked away from her room, no one said a thing until we had turned the first corner and had left Grandma's corridor. Then Wanda beat me to it: "Jase, what in the world did you say to her? I leave when she's almost coming apart in her misery, and I come back a minute or two later and she's all settled down. I can't imagine what you could have said to do that."

"It was something I heard four or five years ago, back in a high-school chapel. It was a chapel talk by a chaplain from Pine Rest, I think. I don't remember too much from my high-school chapels, but he said something that I couldn't get out of my head because it seemed so strange. I didn't understand it then and never did understand it until now. Today I finally understood it."

"Well, come on, are you going to tell us or not?" Wanda said.

"Sure, I'll tell you. It's only five words. Just a little five-word sentence that the chaplain used to close his speech. After he had spoken for twenty minutes or so, he paused and looked out at all of us, cleared his throat a little, and said in kind of a hushed voice: 'Our best memories are prophetic.'" ❦